Equipping the Church: Sexuality, Marriage & Free Speech

SPEAK TRUTH FREELY... WHILE IT'S STILL FREE

Eddie B. Slayton

Copyright © 2014 Eddie B. Slayton

All rights reserved.

ISBN: 150543288X
ISBN 13: 9781505432886
Library of Congress Control Number: 2014921939
CreateSpace Independent Publishing Platform
North Charleston, South Carolina

On October 6, 2014 in a surprise development the US Supreme Court announced it would not accept for review during its current session any of the seven appeals on same-sex marriage bans from five states. The courts' inaction means that the stays placed on lower court decisions in all five states –decisions that struck down bans on marriage for same-sex couples— are immediately lifted, making way for lower courts to issue orders requiring the states to stop enforcing their bans and begin issuing marriage licenses.

In the annals of human history the solution to every moral problem encountered by mankind was arrived at after someone found the courage to *speak truth freely*. And so it will be with America as our nation grapple with the challenges facing us. This book is intended to be read and discussed in a small study group setting either at the church building or in the home. Discussion quesitons appear at the end of each chapter. If you are reading it outside of this setting, please consider sharing the book with the leaders of your congregation; and/or inviting a small group of members to join you in a study.

The US Supreme Court is waiting to see if the winds will continue to blow in the direction toward popular support for same-sex marriage. The court's 2015 - 2016 session is only one short year away (from this writing). Time is of the essence. If a counter-wind is to blow, all Christians must unite in one voice and declare to the nation, and to the US Supreme Court that God's natural law for marriage is above man's highest law.

Truth: the actual state of a matter; conformity with fact or reality; a verified or indisputable fact, proposition, principle, or the like. *(Random House)*

In spite of the relativistic world in which we live, where it's fashionable to believe that *your truth* may be different from mine, absolute truth still exists. Relativism is the theory that all criteria of judgment are relative, varying with individuals and their environments. Such a worldview allows humans the freedom to validate any of their wildest imaginings.

This book is intended to profoundly refute this fallacious theory and is dedicated to the proposition that there is objective truth. Furthermore, this truth is independent of humankind and predates the creation of man.

*Jesus said to him, "**I am the way, the truth, and the life**. No one comes to the Father except through me"* (John 14:6 [NKJV]).

CONTENTS

Foreword		ix
Introduction		xxiii
Chapter 1:	Whatever Happened to Free Speech?	1
Chapter 2:	Homophobia	10
Chapter 3:	Sexual Orientation	21
Chapter 4:	A Mother's Love	35
Chapter 5:	Outing Christians	49
Chapter 6:	Homosexuality: Human Rights and Human Wrongs	62
Chapter 7:	GRANDparents	76
Chapter 8:	Young and Restless	85
Chapter 9:	In Conclusion: Who Will Go?	98
Chapter 10:	Greater Works than These	108

FOREWORD

The First Amendment to the US Constitution *prohibits the making of any law respecting an establishment of religion, impeding the free exercise of religion,* **abridging the freedom of speech, infringing on the freedom of the press,** *interfering with the right to peaceably assemble or prohibiting the petitioning for a governmental redress of grievances.* It was adopted on December 15, 1791 as one of the ten amendments that comprise the Bill of Rights.

I have chosen to use my freedom of speech to write a book that highlights God's truth about one sin: **homosexuality**. I realize that some people will ask, why write a book highlighting homosexuality? They will seek to invalidate such an effort simply because there are so many other sins. In fact, some of these people may ask you the very same question. Consider this reply: "Are you saying there should be no books highlighting any sin, or that there should be a book to highlight all the other sins, too?" To the former I suggest replying, "Ridiculous," and politely dismissing them, and to the latter, "If you write the next book, I will gladly read it after I finish this one."

Sin began in Genesis, chapter 3, with the fall of man after the lie told in the garden: *Then the serpent said to the woman, "You will not surely die"* (Gen. 3:4 [NKJV]). There were three steps in man's original sin:

Man heard a lie.
Man believed a lie.
Man obeyed a lie.

Correspondingly, there are three steps in man's restoration:

Man must hear the truth.
Man must believe the truth.
Man must obey the truth.

Homosexuals have shunned God's truth and embraced Satan's lies. Today in the United States, we are not free to speak God's truth about homosexuality without meeting a swift response from those advocating for this sinful lifestyle. Below are some responses encountered by people who recently dared to *speak truth freely*.

On June 16, 2012, while on the syndicated radio talk show, *The Ken Coleman Show*, Chick-fil-A president and chief operating officer (COO), Dan Cathy, stated: "I think we are inviting God's judgment on our nation when we shake our fist at Him and say, 'We know better than you as to what constitutes a marriage.' I pray God's mercy on our generation that has such a prideful, arrogant attitude to think that we have the audacity to define what marriage is about."

The following month, on July 2, *Biblical Recorder* published an interview with Dan Cathy, who was asked about opposition to his company's "support of the traditional family." He replied, "Well, guilty as charged." Cathy continued, "We are very much supportive of the family—the biblical definition of the family unit. We are a family-owned business, a family-led business, and we are married to our first wives. We give God thanks for that…we want to do anything we possibly can to strengthen families. We are very much committed to that," Cathy emphasized. "We intend to stay the course," he said. "We know that it might not be popular with everyone, but thank the Lord, we live in a country where we can share our values and operate on biblical principles."

Backlash

In response to the July 2 interview, the Jim Henson Company, which had entered its *Pajanimals* in a kids' meal toy licensing arrangement in 2011, said that it would cease its business relationship with Chick-fil-A and donate payment for the brand to Gay & Lesbian Alliance Against Defamation (GLAAD). Citing safety concerns, Chick-fil-A stopped distributing the toys. A spokeswoman stated the decision had been made on July 19 and was unrelated to the controversy.

In August 2012, progressive groups delivered petitions with over eighty thousand signatures to publisher HarperCollins demanding that the publisher cut plans to include *Berenstain Bears* titles as part of a kids' meal promotion. Upon being presented with petitions demanding that *Berenstain Bears* be pulled from a Chick-fil-A promotion, HarperCollins issued a statement saying, "We have a long history of diversity and inclusiveness and work tirelessly to protect the freedom of expression. It is not our practice to cancel a contract with an author, or any other party, for exercising *their first amendment rights.*"

Students at several colleges and universities launched efforts to ban or remove the company's restaurants from their campuses. On November 3, 2011, the New York University Student Senators Council voted nineteen to four to retain the Chick-fil-A franchise on campus. This vote came prior to a petition with over eleven thousand signatures opposing its presence on campus was sent to the student council.

On February 28, 2012, the Northeastern University (NU) student senate passed a resolution to cancel plans for a Chick-fil-A franchise on campus, stating that "the student body does not support bringing CFA [Chick-fil-A] to campus," and "Student concerns reflected CFA's history of donating to antigay organizations." The restaurant chain was finalizing a contract to bring it to NU when students protested. Other forms of protest occurred. Gay rights activists organized a "Kiss Off" to occur on August 3, an event where LGBT (lesbian, bisexual, gay, transgendered) individuals would show affection in public, but it attracted smaller-than-hoped-for crowds.

On August 15, 2012, a gunman attempted to enter the Washington, DC headquarters of the Family Research Council, carrying fifteen Chick-fil-A sandwiches, a 9-mm handgun, and a box of ammunition. He shot a security guard in the left arm, and, following his arrest, he told police that he wanted to use the sandwiches to "make a statement against the people who work in that building...and with their stance against gay rights and Chick-fil-A," and that he planned "to kill as many people as I could...then smear a Chicken-fil-A sandwich on their face."

In response to the controversy, former Arkansas Governor Mike Huckabee initiated a Chick-fil-A Appreciation Day movement to counter a boycott of Chick-fil-A launched by same-sex marriage activists. More than six hundred thousand people RSVP'd on Facebook for Huckabee's appreciation event. On August 1, Chick-fil-A restaurants experienced a large show of public support across the nation, with the company reporting record-breaking sales. A consulting firm projected that the average Chick-fil-A restaurant increased sales by 29.9 percent and had 367 more customers than a typical Wednesday.

Miami Dolphins

In May 2014 the Miami Dolphins fined safety Don Jones for tweeting a negative comment about openly gay draft pick, Michael

Foreword

Sam, and then ordered him to "educational training" to learn sensitivity. Mr. Jones tweeted, "OMG" and "horrible" after Mr. Sam turned to his male partner during the televised national draft pick event and exchanged a big kiss.

Although Jones deleted the tweets, the public relations damage was already done. He quickly sent out a statement of apology for what he said were "inappropriate comments" he made on social media.

His statement: "I take full responsibility for them, and I regret that these tweets took away from his draft moment. I remember last year when I was drafted in the seventh round and all of the emotions and happiness I felt when I received the call that gave me an opportunity to play for an NFL team, and I wish him all the best in his NFL career. I sincerely apologize to Mr. Ross [owner Stephen M. Ross], my teammates, coaches, staff, and fans for these tweets. I am committed to represent the values of the Miami Dolphins organization and appreciate the opportunity I have been given to do so going forward."

The coach of the Dolphins, Joe Philbin, said the organization was "disappointed" to see Mr. Jones's tweets. He also said that "we met with Don today about respect, discrimination, and judgment. These comments are not consistent with the values and standards of our program. We will continue to emphasize and educate our players that these statements will not be tolerated." According to published reports, Mr. Jones was banned from all team activities until he attended and finished "educational training" to address the matter.

Next, the following is a legislative account of a California law passed in 2012 (no personal commentary is included in the account):

California Senate Bill No. 1172   Chapter 835

An act to add Article 15 (commencing with Section 865) to Chapter 1 of Division 2 of the Business and Professions Code, relating to healing arts.

[Approved by Governor September 30, 2012. Filed with Secretary of State September 30, 2012.]

Legislative Counsel's Digest, SB 1172, Lieu. Sexual orientation change efforts.

Existing law provides for licensing and regulation of various professions in the healing arts, including physicians and surgeons, psychologists, marriage and family therapists, educational psychologists, clinical social workers, and licensed professional clinical counselors.

This bill would prohibit a mental health provider, as defined, from engaging in sexual orientation change efforts, as defined, with a patient under eighteen years of age. The bill would provide that any sexual orientation change efforts attempted on a patient under eighteen years of age by a mental health provider shall be considered unprofessional conduct and shall subject the provider to discipline by the provider's licensing entity.

Beverly Press: Lieu praises SB 1172 ruling.

February 20, 2014

California State Sen. Ted Lieu (D-Torrance), the author of SB 1172, which repealed the practice of gay conversion therapy for minors, praised a Jan. 29th Ninth Circuit Court ruling denying a rehearing in a lawsuit that challenged his law. "Supporters of equal rights can now rest more easily," Lieu said. "Today's

Foreword

decision is cement over the nail in the coffin of the bogus practice of 'reparative' therapy."

End of legislative account.

In case you missed this saga, as a result of California SB 1172, parents of children under age eighteen will not be able to get professional counseling for a child who is having **unwanted** same-sex attractions. If a licensed counselor performs such counseling, he or she risks losing his or her license to practice in the state of California.

There is a chance that you missed the reports surrounding Chick-fil-A, the Miami Dolphins, or SB 1172; but, if you've been on planet earth for the past three years, it has been impossible to miss the gay-marriage movement. Thirty-one US state constitutional amendments banning legal recognition of same-sex unions have been adopted. At present, more than a dozen federal and state judges have struck down part or all of state-level bans in recent months. As of this writing, after more than twenty consecutive federal rulings against same-sex marriage bans, the Louisiana ban was upheld.

If you are not shocked and awed by these events, you are certain to be after what comes next. As unbelievable as it may sound, it is real. All of the following information comes from the publisher (no personal commentary is included):

The Queen James Bible Paperback—November 27, 2012

www.queenjamesbible.com Available for purchase at Amazon.com

A Gay Bible

The Queen James Bible is based on the King James Bible, edited to prevent homophobic misinterpretation.

Homosexuality in the Bible

Homosexuality was first mentioned in the Bible in 1946 in the Revised Standard Version. There is no mention of, or reference to, homosexuality in any Bible prior to this—only interpretations have been made. Anti-LGBT Bible interpretations commonly cite only eight verses in the Bible that they interpret to mean homosexuality is a sin—eight verses in a book of thousands!

The Queen James Bible seeks to resolve **interpretive ambiguity** in the Bible as it pertains to homosexuality: We edited those eight verses in a way that makes homophobic interpretations impossible.

Who is Queen James?

The King James Bible is the most popular Bible of all time and arguably the most important English language document of all time. It is the brainchild and namesake of King James I, who wanted an English language Bible that all could own and read. The KJV, as it is called, has been in print for over four hundred years and has brought more people to Christ than any other Bible translation. Commonly known to biographers, but often surprising to most Christians, King James I was a well-known bisexual. Though he did marry a woman, his many gay relationships were so well-known that, among some of his friends and court, he was known as "Queen James." It is in his great debt and honor that we name the Queen James Bible so.

A Fabulous Bible

The QJB is a big, fabulous Bible. It is printed and bound in the United States on thick, high-quality paper in a beautiful, readable typeface. It is the perfect Bible for ceremony, study, sermon, gift-giving, or simply to put on display in the home or church.

Foreword

You can't choose your sexuality, but you can choose Jesus. Now you can choose a Bible, too.

For God so loved the world, that he gave his only begotten Son, that whosoever believeth in him should not perish, but have everlasting life (John 3:16 [NKJV]).

End of Queen James Bible account.

Our nation has changed and is continuing to change at an astounding pace. Today (2014), virtually every American citizen is keenly aware that the truth (God's word) is perceived as anti-gay speech; and speaking the truth is no longer free. There is now a price to pay whenever someone speaks the truth about homosexuality. The winds of change have been blowing for a while now, and if you dare to speak truth freely, it is certain that you will be shouted down.

Homosexuality is but one of the many immoral ills that are degrading our nation. The proverbial question in times of crisis is, how did we get here? Some are convinced that we are here because we took prayer out of the schools; others believe we're still reaping the fruits of the 1960s drug culture or the blurring of gender roles with stay-at-home dads in the 1980s. Still others are convinced that the favorable media depictions of the gay lifestyle and the proliferation of sexually explicit content are to blame.

This book was created upon the stance that there is one reason that evil thrives: **righteous people stop speaking against it with the truth.** *Sanctify them through thy truth: thy word is truth* (John 17:17 [KJV]).

As people of faith, our mission is first to learn the truth, obey it, and then vigorously defend it in the face of attacks. Sadly, too many self-identified Christians do not know what the scriptures teach about many of the sinful social ills plaguing our nation. How many of us can give *book, chapter, and verse* explaining God's position on: homosexuality, gambling, social drinking, or premarital sex? Therefore, we are left trying to refute the world's opinions with our opinions, which is the best we can do if we have not spirituality matured to the point of hiding God's word in our hearts.

*For though by this time you ought to be teachers, you need someone to teach you again the first principles of the oracles of God; and you have come to need milk and not solid food. For everyone who partakes only of milk is **unskilled in the word of righteousness**, for he is a babe. But solid food belongs to those who are of full age, that is, those who **by reason of use** have their senses exercised to discern both good and evil.*

*Therefore, leaving the discussion of the elementary principles of Christ, **let us go on to maturity**, not laying again the foundation of repentance from dead works and of faith toward God* (Heb. 5:12–6:1 [NKJV]).

The previous passages, along with many others in the Bible, are a clear indication that Christians are commanded to grow. Prolonged spiritual immaturity is not an option for anyone who wears the name *Christian*. Every parent expects his or her child to learn and grow, and God expects his children to do likewise. God has this expectation because he knows the perils of not growing. Failure to grow in God's word makes it harder to live a life of faithful obedience and lessens our ability to make a positive impact on the world. And, our American culture is reaping the fruits of *little to no positive moral impact* by people of faith over the past few decades.

Morality is defined as "conformity to the rules of right conduct." Historically, morality in the United States was biblically based. However, the last couple of generations have brought many redefinitions. Situational ethics have removed biblical authority as the standard for "right rules of conduct" and replaced the Bible with one's own personal preferences. As a result, our nation is now engulfed in a moral revolution. A moral revolution requires three things:

1. What was previously condemned is now celebrated,
2. What was previously celebrated is now condemned, and
3. Those who refuse to celebrate are condemned.

Ample evidence of this moral revolution is seen in the state of marriage in American culture: divorce, cohabitation, same-sex marriage, and other trends. At present our nation sits squarely in stage three of the current moral revolution. This chapter began with just a few of the recent events in which those who dared to speak God's truth were condemned.

Yet, in spite of the tenets of political correctness, God is still the ultimate authority, and his Word is the ultimate truth for humans. And when one has studied and proven oneself to be *"a workman who needeth not to be ashamed"* (2 Tim. 2:15), one's opinions will be consistent with scripture. Therefore, when equipped, a faithful disciple of Christ will be able to refute worldly opinions with scriptural truth and the opposing party's disagreement will be with God.

The aim of this writing is to awaken God's people from their silent slumber. In spite of the present challenges, the war is far from over. In fact, the victory has already been secured. The scriptures are filled with examples where it appeared that God's people faced insurmountable odds and an unconquerable foe. In every instance God's position was consistent:

If my people who are called by my name will humble themselves, and pray and seek my face, and turn from their wicked ways, then I will hear from heaven, and will forgive their sin and heal their land (2 Chron. 7:14 [NKJV]).

Righteousness exalts a nation: but sin is a reproach to any people (Prov. 14:34 [KJV]).

Many Christians feel powerless against the tide of evil that has invaded our land. Sadly, some have strayed, not necessarily by participating in such evil but by lacking the courage to speak God's truth freely.

Like the ten spies in Numbers, chapter 13, too many Christians are afraid to speak his truth, leaving some to wonder if they see themselves as *grasshoppers* in the eyes of homosexual advocates. But throughout the Bible, God demonstrates that he doesn't need a majority to overcome evil.

This book is written to equip and provide a platform for the Joshuas and Calebs who believe "we are well able" (Num. 13:30) to be victorious if we are willing to speak God's truth freely. The book is designed to be a resource that's used in a twelve-week Bible class. The material is written to be read, understood, and discussed at the high school to adult level.

The book provides a sound, unedited, scriptural foundation of God's view of homosexuality and shines the light of truth on several of the erroneous positions utilized by those advocating for this sinful lifestyle. We are living in an age when these errors are represented as truth by the media and others. Unfortunately, some Christians have become disheartened and confused. They simply need to be reminded that no lie on earth can stand against the truth found in God's Word.

The greatest threat to a moral society is *inattention*; you must *attend* to morality in order to retain it.

Speak truth freely, while it's still free.

STUDY GUIDE

Study Group Ground Rules

This study group is designed for Christians to engage in a discussion surrounding the issues raised in the book *Equipping the Church: Sexuality, Marriage & Free Speech*. If our nation is to make gains in undoing the damage done to God's design for the home, the movement must begin with God's people having open and frank discussions aimed at building unity within the fold. Inevitably there will be disagreements; however, everyone will at all times remain respectful, will make every attempt not to repeat comments made by others within group discussions, and will at no time repeat a comment and directly or indirectly attribute it to the speaker. These discussions are to be considered private and confidential; any violation is construed as a personal violation of trust.

Foreword

Recent Events:

> Chick-fil-A   Miami Dolphins
> Same Sex Marriage Movement   SB 1172
> The Queen James Bible   Other events

Discuss the significance of these events and the deeper implications beneath them.

Do you feel constrained at all in your ability to speak truth freely? If so, under what circumstances, and how do you feel about that?

What are some of the reasons people believe we're going through the current changes?

Do you agree or disagree with the stance upon which this book was created?

What is going to happen when you refute homosexuality with your opinion?

Why would scripture be better than your opinion?

What are the three steps needed for a moral revolution?

What is some evidence that the United States is in step three?

Discus what it means to attend to morality.

Personal take away:

_____

_____

_____

INTRODUCTION

Many Christians fail to understand or fully comprehend why anyone would want to engage in homosexual activity. To some, the very idea is either puzzling or repugnant. Below is a perspective that you may very well have never contemplated. Consider what it might be like to have urges and yearnings for as long as you can remember, while everything in the natural world is telling you that you dare not express or act on them.

The following story is an anonymous account of one person's journey in coming to terms with homosexuality:

> I suppose I have always seen myself as a burden for some reason. I was the youngest in the household, the one needing care and attention when others really needed it more… so I got good at just being me…not being helped by anyone, keeping things to myself, not talking, just dealing with things independently.
>
> I don't know when I realized I was gay. I think it was around the age of sixteen. It wasn't until I turned eighteen that I decided it wasn't going to go away, and I needed to start accepting that was who I was. I got really depressed, scared, angry, and felt totally alone through those two years. The mental stress and pressure built up so much that I needed to do something.

I remember one day flicking through the white pages. I wasn't really looking for a number. I was just bored. I found a telephone number under a counseling heading near the front of the book. It said, "Gay and Lesbian Counseling Line: 4:00 p.m.–midnight."

I needed to talk to someone, not friends or family. I needed to talk to someone I didn't know, so I called the counseling line. I remember calling all but the last digit of the phone number and then hanging up because I was too scared—I did this ten or more times. I didn't know what was going to happen; I didn't even know if I could talk to a stranger.

To be truthful, I didn't end up calling that day, but the following day I forced myself to. I called and talked to the guy on the counseling line for about forty-five minutes. At first, my fears were that the person on the other end of the phone wouldn't be able to do anything to help or wouldn't take me seriously or would tell me that I was wrong and needed to change my (gay-related) feelings.

I must have sounded really scared when we started talking, and he somehow got me to calm down a bit, and then about halfway through the conversation he said to me, "You sound a lot better already," and I was feeling a lot better. He gave me some telephone numbers for my local area and told me about a support group in my city for gay/bisexual men. I told him that I couldn't do that (go to a support group), but I would call the numbers he gave me. He was the first person I ever told I was gay.

After about two weeks, I got the courage to call the number, and the guy there told me there was a support group for gay youth in my area. I told him I couldn't go; it was hard enough for me to just call him to start with. He gave me heaps of

Introduction

encouragement and told me the phone number of the guy who runs a local youth group for young gay and bisexual guys. I called right away, but it wasn't until after about a month that I went to the youth group for the first time.

To this day I can still remember how hard it was. I had that nervous, sick feeling in my stomach the whole day, right up to after the group started. The group has done so much good for me. It helped me break down the stereotypes that I assumed all gay people were (or had to be). I have made some good friends from the group. I can talk to others about being gay, and they understand.

If I hadn't gone to the group to begin with, I would never have gotten to know the guy I now think of as my closest friend. He was the first gay friend I ever made, and, whether he knows it or not, he has helped me through some really difficult times. Just being there as a friend, as someone to talk to.

Going to the youth group was the best thing I ever did for myself; it makes me so happy that I got the courage to go. I look back to the time before I went to the group, how unhappy and miserable I was with myself and my life. Being around other gay people has helped me accept myself more and more. I am now at the point where I am starting to feel good about myself and good about life in general.

Sometimes things get tough in my life, as they do in everyone's at some point or another. When things get really tough, I have a habit of digging my heels in and proclaiming independence. All I want to do is go it alone. "I am not weak—I don't need others!" my head shouts at me. But I have found that sometimes it's important to not go it alone.

I have a habit of hiding. When things get tough, I hide from the people I care about so that I don't hurt them or burden them or something. I don't want my stuff causing them to feel bad, so it's just easier to hide from it all—from all the pressures and stressors of people—and somehow it seems the safe option.

I am starting to learn that when you are really down, or your life just goes crazy, it's sometimes important to reach out to understanding people, even when it's easier just to distance yourself and hide. I have a couple of people I can reach out to, and I know that they have people they in turn can talk to about things. Sometimes it is more comforting for these people if I honestly tell them what is going on rather than if I just hide from them entirely.

Throughout the last generation, stories similar to this have occurred a million times over. Obviously the issue of homosexuality is multifaceted and cannot be distilled down to a single factor. However, we most certainly can look at the current cultural context and point to at least one major contributing factor to the permissively immoral climate in which we now live: *divorce.*

The current demands to redefine marriage to include homosexual couples are a consequence of the redefinition of marriage stemming from heterosexuals divorce. Though they cite the very desire to marry as evidence that their sexual behavior is not inherently promiscuous, homosexual activist Andrew Sullivan acknowledge that gays want the right to marry only because of the promiscuity permitted in modern marriage:

"The world of no-strings heterosexual hookups and 50 percent divorce rates preceded gay marriage," he points out. "All homosexuals are saying is that, *under the current definition,* there's no reason to exclude us. If you want to return *straight* marriage to

Introduction

the 1950s, go ahead. *But until you do,* the exclusion of gays…is a denial of basic civil equality." Sullivan and others do not want traditional monogamous marriage, only marriage as transformed by easily accessible divorce.

It is said that nature *abhors a vacuum,* meaning that whenever space is vacated, something will move in to fill the void. Our purpose here is not to have a philosophical consideration of how this premise plays out in the physical world; on the other hand, we will consider its application to the spiritual world. Over the last thirty or forty years, God's people, Christians, have joined with the world in devaluing God's holy institution of marriage. "No-fault divorce" has created a climate in which the marriage commitment is now equivalent to Walmart's policy: *return it for any reason.*

The divorce rate for Christians has grown to the point where it is comparable to the *rank sinner.* And in so doing, Christians have contributed mightily to the carnage of brokenness left in its wake. What did we think was going to fill the spiritual void created when we demonstrated to ourselves, and to the world, that we no longer truly believed that God's holy design of **one man, one woman, for life** was applicable to, or possible for, us? And now, like first graders, we want to run and tattle to God about the despicable things **"they"** are doing. Maybe God is saying to us, *Get the beam out of your eye first* (Matt. 7:5 [KJV]).

No-fault divorce has contributed greatly to the cultural context that accelerated the devaluing of marriage in America. While this was happening, the Internet and the proliferation of personal electronic devices made pornography as accessible as checking today's weather report. It is within this setting that *sexting* (Google it if you don't know what it means) by teens and preteens has flourished alongside a significant increase in adolescent and young-adult sexual assault.

In such a cultural climate, is anyone really surprised that homosexuals feel that they can lay a legitimate claim to marriage? In public debate and private conversation, they have challenged Christians from the position of, considering Christian's recent performance in marriage, why not give them a chance at it? And frankly, it can be rather challenging to fashion a proper response.

If you find yourself faced with replying to such a question, consider admitting that they are right; because they are. The human carnage left in the wake of millions of divorces (including many Christians) has contributed to the cultural climate that is now increasingly turning its back on biblical marriage. Fifty years ago many homosexuals lived together as committed couples, but they did not see their relationship as a marriage. But over the past generation, heterosexuals have disrespected marriage through sexual immorality and divorce to the point that homosexuals actually believe that two men can live together in the biblical concept of marriage.

There is an old adage that two wrongs don't make a right. The solution to sin and disobedience to God is never more sin and disobedience. Even if we desire to do so, we do not have the liberty to give our blessings to same-sex marriage. Regardless of how guilty Christians are of contributing to the carnage, their only option is to repent of their sin and lovingly implore that homosexuals do likewise. Our charge is to convince anyone seeking same sex-marriage that God's design is right, regardless of people's misuse and abuse of it.

Sadly God's design has been so twisted and distorted that some Chrisitans cannot confidently put forth a scriptural defense. If this is the case with some of God's people there is little wonder that many in the world believe that same-sex couples have every right to marriage. Every Christian must take the time to pray for courage and study for knowledge to equip him or her self to defend God's design for marriage.

Introduction

The American Heritage Dictionary defines **design** as:

1. to prepare the preliminary sketch or the plans for (a work to be executed), especially to plan the form and structure of:
2. to intend for a definite purpose

Stop here and read Gen. 2:16-25.

One thing that is clear from these scriptures is God is a God of design. There was a particular form and structure to his design process. He created man; man was alone so he created the animal kingdom. There was no one fit for Adam so God created Eve as a helper fit (comparable) for him. Man and woman were not created for the sole purpose of enjoying each other's company. As husband and wife, Adam and Eve were given a particular function: *So God created man in his own image; in the image of God he created him; male and female he created them. Then God blessed them, and God said to them, "Be fruitful and multiply; fill the earth and subdue it; have dominion over the fish of the sea, over the birds of the air, and over every living thing that moves on the earth.* (Gen. 1:27-29 [NKJV])

The problem with marriage today is people are using it for a purpose God never intended. And, when people use marriage for a purpose he never intended the institution will not function as he intended. Same-sex couples are physically incapable of fulfilling the basic function intended by God: *procreation*. Furthermore, no matter how strongly two men declare their love for one another they cannot have the mutually gratifying physical and spiritual relationship God intended for a man and a woman.

If our nation is going to restore its belief in God and his design for marriage and the family, Christians must get their collective houses in order. We must practice what we preach. The last generation has shown us that the world was watching us, and in some respects that it has followed our lead. By the same token, if Christians repent and get their homes in order, it will show the world that God's justice system works. His justice system makes restoration available to every repentant sinner: both the heterosexual sinner and the homosexual sinner. The foundation of God's justice is love, and he expects love to be the foundation for Christians as we grapple with our human relationships.

*Jesus said to him, "You shall love the L*ORD *your God with all your heart, with all your soul, and with all your mind. This is the first and great commandment. And the second is like it:* **You shall love your neighbor as yourself**" (Matt. 22:37–39 [NKJV]).

What if your neighbor is a thief or prostitute or alcoholic…or, heaven forbid, what if your neighbor is a member of the LGBT community? What type of sin will allow you to get an exemption from the charge to love them? And if you didn't love them, how close would you get to them? And if you don't get close to them, what are the chances that you will ever get an opportunity to share the gospel with them? And if you don't share the gospel with them, what chance will they have of repenting, turning from their sin, and accepting God's offer of salvation?

But wait, what if you develop a close relationship with them, share the gospel with them, and they refuse to obey and continue in their sin; do you have to keep on loving them? Be careful here; your answer will determine whether you think God meant for your love to be "conditional" or "unconditional." (Hint: the correct answer is the same as God's expectation for the way Christian brothers and sisters are to love one another)

We are called to *love our neighbor as ourselves.* We must honor and esteem all people and must wrong and injure none; we must have a good will towards all, and as we have the opportunity, we must do good to all. We must love our neighbor as ourselves,

Introduction

as truly and sincerely as we love ourselves. In many instances this may mean that we must deny ourselves for the good of our neighbor, we must make ourselves servants to the true welfare of others, and be willing to spend and be spent for them.

The current generation of practicing Christians seems to have lost site of the primary goal of Christianity: *to save the world, not condemn it.* How can any Christian have the authority to do something that God wouldn't do: *For God did not send his Son into the world to condemn the world, but that the world through him might be saved* (John 3:17 [NKJV]). We must be unapologetically biblical. However, the goal is not to make the homosexual straight so he or she can go to hell as a heterosexual. The goal is to lead him or her to Christ so he or she can live a rihteous life.

Some Christians have been taken in by the world's assertion that "Love = Acceptance." What is meant by this is that, if you love the person, you are compelled to accept their sins. Nothing could be further from the truth. By way of example, how many of us die-hard sports fans love someone who is a fan of our team's arch enemy (Celtics, Lakers; Alabama, Auburn; Duke, North Carolina; Yankees, Red Sox)? Even if you are in a loving relationship with that person for seventy-five years, you will never, ever embrace the team that he or she loves and you hate. *Unconditional love is not unconditional acceptance.* Bottom line: in order to love our sinful neighbor, we must develop a heart so full of love for God and humankind that we are able to see our fellow man with our left eye while simultaneously seeing God with our right eye.

If you read the story above and your heart was not touched, not even a little bit, by the turmoil and pain that this young man is going through, you may not be ready to read this book. Homosexuality is sin, and beginning with chapter 1, we will deal with the issue in its entirety. But, the first issue for you is, do you have a compassionate heart? In order to feel compassion for someone, we must first be able to see ourselves in a similar condition. We call this empathy: *the ability of understanding and imaginatively entering into another person's feelings (Random House Dictionary).*

Without compassion and empathy, the best you can do is browbeat others with scriptures from your lofty perch atop your personal bully pulpit. Without compassion and empathy, your battle cry is, "God hates sin; I am standing with God!" For those who choose to take this position, it might get a little tough for you to hold on to:

Do you not know that the unrighteous will not inherit the kingdom of God? Do not be deceived. Neither fornicators, nor idolaters, nor adulterers, nor homosexuals nor sodomites, nor thieves, nor covetous, nor drunkards, nor revilers, nor extortionistsers will inherit the kingdom of God. **And such were some of you.** *But you were washed, but you were sanctified, but you were justified in the name of the Lord Jesus and by the Spirit of our God* (1 Cor. 6:9–11 [NKJV]).

For there is no difference; **for all have sinned** *and fall short of the glory of God, being justified freely by His grace through the redemption that is in Christ Jesus* (Rom. 3:22–24 [NKJV]).

So when they continued asking Him, He raised Himself up and said to them, **"He who is without sin"** *among you, let him throw a stone at her first." And again he stooped down and wrote on the ground* (John 8:7–8 [NKJV]).

In an interview a Christian who had previously lived life as a lesbian was asked the question, "What is it that the church doesn't get about the LGBT community?" The reply was, "That they desperately need to be embraced by the church community. We must accept them with all the other sinners and love, support and nurture them too." To do so would be following the example of Jesus: *And when the scribes and Pharisees saw him eating with the tax collectors and sinners, they said to His disciples, "How is it that he eats and drinks with tax collectors and sinners?"* (Mark 2:16 [NKJV]).

Like all of us, their *big* sin is unbelief and disobedience to God; that and everything else will get taken care of in the water of baptism by the blood of Jesus. We must shift our primary focus from their *sexual orientations* to their *soul orientations*. For a Christian, what is the difference between lust that emanates from same-sex attraction and lust from heterosexual attraction? We must learn to teach and lead them without shaming them. **It is never going to be their fault that we are not spiritually mature enough to do this.**

We are all captives in these *tabernacles of flesh* and all in need of God's compassion and mercy. It behooves none of us to withhold an outstretched hand to the least of us. Yes, homosexuality is sin, and those caught up in its web are in need of deliverance, repentance, and salvation. But we must first recognize their humanity and recognize their personalities. We must recognize that they have dreams, hopes, and aspirations.

All of us are searching for a life that provides an opportunity to display our highest and best and then to experience the peace and joy of having done so. It's only from the vantage point of one human being to another that their hearts and ears will become open, and they will then have an opportunity to hear what we have to say. Our message to them is that there is only one way to experience true peace and lasting joy: living one's life in obedience to God. The love, acceptance, and fulfillment that they are seeking in the flesh cannot be compared with the joy that's only found in an obedient, harmonious relationship with God the father through Jesus Christ, His Son.

Their greatest need is for you, as compassionately as you can, **to speak truth freely**.

STUDY GUIDE

Introduction

Did you feel any compassion for the main character in the story? If not, is that all right?

What is the difference between sympathy and empathy?

Should a Christian empathize with the person in the story? Why or why not?

When done by others, what is the BIG sin that is hard for you to stomach?

As it relates to being sinful, what is the difference between homosexual lust and heterosexual lust?

Are we all captives in *tabernacles of flesh* and all in need of God's compassion and mercy? Give scriptural support for your answer.

Do you agree or disagree with the assertion that Christians have contributed to the current cultural devaluation of the biblical model of marriage? Defend your position.

If you believe that Christians have contributed to the devaluation, should we give in to same-sex marriage and give them a chance? Why or why not?

Describe the form and structure to God's design process for humankind.

Do you think that God's holy design of *one man, one woman for life* is still possible? Why or why not?

Did God intend for your love for your neighbor to be conditional or unconditional? Why?

Have you ever struggled with sin in your life that you eventually overcame? (Only share as much as you are comfortable sharing.)

How do you think your congregation *should* (not would), should respond to someone who repents of the sin of homosexuality and is struggling to be free of it?

Personal take away:

_____

_____

_____

Chapter 1
WHATEVER HAPPENED TO FREE SPEECH?

History is littered with atrocious examples of human's inhumanity to other humans. Two of the most horrific examples are the evils committed during the Jewish Holocaust and the African slave trade. These events provide a cautionary tale of the extent to which humankind may mistreat one another when driven by unrestrained fear, hatred, and greed.

As a new nation, America was physically built upon the backs of forced human labor during the period of the slave trade. Yet, as a nation we matured and now stand as an unrivaled proponent and defender of human rights and human dignity.

Our nation's founding fathers recognized that love and hate are the universe's most powerful forces. They recognized that both have the power to transform people and thereby the world. With great wisdom they also recognized that true freedom necessitated that humans must be free to express both, and the freedom to do so is secured by the First Amendment to the US Constitution.

The pendulum of free and open expression of ideas in America is always swinging. The arc for the pendulum currently is, and has always been, public opinion. You are either embraced or shunned depending upon the degree to which the ideas you express agree with or oppose the prevailing views of the day.

As it relates to the expression of ideas surrounding homosexuality the pendulum has swung drastically in the last generation. Just thirty years ago, in 1984, it would have been most unusual for someone to stand in an open public forum and defend the position that two men have the same rights in a marital relationship as a man and a woman.

Today (2014) you'd be hard pressed to find a politician (Democrat or Republican) who will stand and even suggest the idea that two men have no marital rights. And not many people will express this viewpoint except within the safe confines of their religious or social group, and perhaps, not even then, unless this is the unquestioned position within the group.

We have arrived at this particular point in time with some dark history as our backdrop. *We have seen the enemy, and the enemy is us.* Throughout human history, pendulums sometimes receive their initial push toward justice by people who see a wrong and are sincerely trying to right that wrong. Many wrongs have been committed against people simply because they lived a homosexual life. Our nation stood silently while those who lived this lifestyle were harassed, beaten, defamed, and discriminated against.

However, there are always unintended consequences of every action. In fact, the laws of nature have seen to that: "for every action there is an equal and opposite reaction." Over the course of the last generation, many millions of nonhomosexual people have supported the effort to stop the mistreatment of those who embrace this life. In the process of eliminating the wrongs committed against homosexuals, the advocates for the homosexual community have *stolen* some undeserved rights.

Whatever Happened To Free Speech?

And now as a nation, we find ourselves engulfed in a state of perplexity or uncertainty, especially as to what to do. Do we speak against homosexuality and risk being aligned with those who spew hatred and bigotry? Or do we remain silent? When large numbers of people remain silent on an issue to which they harbor deeply felt opposition, at some point they will speak. The universal question is, "What will be the cost of their silence?"

Our great nation was built on "*speech*" that grew out of a period during which the cost of our silence became intolerable. Revolution is often the mode of expression for a people who endure a period where their voice (speech) is suppressed. America is big enough and strong enough to survive hate speech and love speech; whenever we stifle either, we stifle the very ideal upon which America was built.

It is best to speak respectfully and to speak from an informed position. But I am prepared to defend to my death your right to speak ignorantly and disrespectfully. Human history has shown us that real danger does not lie in our speech; on the contrary, the true danger lies in our **silence**.

Throughout human history silence as a public response in the face of evil inevitably was resolved in crisis. In the politically correct and media-driven culture in which we live, the word "crisis" is so overused that it has lost its ability to mobilize us to act. Homosexual advocates have reframed the public view of their illicit sexual activity from God's descriptions of "sodomy" and those who practice such as "sodomites" to the most pleasing of terms: "a gay lifestyle."

For years Hollywood, the media, and some political leaders have been coopted to help push their agenda for acceptance. Unfortunately, many leaders who resisted this movement have been replaced by sympathizers whose inactions have led to undermining the home and demoralizing the nation. As a result some sodomy laws are relaxed, while others have been eliminated.

The challenge for people of faith is to hold on to God's view of their condition. God views homosexual acts as an abomination and deviant, unnatural behavior (Lev. 18:22, Rom. 1:26–8). Can one not see the politically correct crowd grimacing as these scriptures are read and proclaimed? Can one hear their objections: "Do not use the word 'sodomites.'" "Do not say 'homosexual'—use the word 'gay' or the phrase 'alternative lifestyle.'" Has our politically correct culture caused your view to become blurred? Do you see them as sodomites or nice people who are simply living out their natural sexual orientation? In 2014 this is the politically correct viewpoint.

Political correctness (PC) is one of the greatest threats to morality for our nation and the whole world. PC demands a total disregard for right and wrong. It denies the very existence of an objective standard of morality, decency, and righteousness. Furthermore, PC would have you believe there is no absolute standard of right and wrong. It would have everyone be a law unto themselves—the mantra of the day is "If it feels good, just do it!"

How did we get to where we are today? Who could have imagined that our society would become so indifferent toward godless and immoral behavior? How in the world is it even possible that America is now supporting, promoting, protecting, and defending the very sin that destroyed the cities of Sodom and Gomorrah (Gen. 19:1–27)? Our nation is in a downward spiral that is gaining momentum every single day that we silently go about our business.

Our apathy and complacency is allowing the homosexual agenda to grow and thrive. Where are the moral and upright citizens of this land? Where are the so-called "Christians" who are supposed to be the majority in this country? Their voices are as silent as a still wind. Many are afraid of "political correctness." They don't want to be viewed as being out of step with the times. They are afraid of being thought of as bigots, extremists, and fanatics. Friends, your fear is misplaced: *And fear not them which kill the body, but are not able to kill the soul: but rather fear him which is able to destroy both soul and body in hell* (Matt. 10:28 [NKJV]).

Whenever an evil age goes unchallenged by the righteous, the last foe to defeat is God. As a result of their evil deeds and unwillingness to repent, evildoers resolve to the position of hating God. They hate him because he condemns their sinful behavior. They hate him because he demands that they turn from their sin and live an upright and moral life. But they refuse to live a righteous life; yet they still want to be free from condemnation by God and humans.

They demand their right to live as they so choose, which God gives everyone the free will to do. As long as we live in this world, we have the freedom to live as we want. But there is a day of reckoning coming. Every human being will one day stand before the Lord to be judged for the things done in their body: *Rejoice, O young man, in thy youth; and let thy heart cheer thee in the days of thy youth, and walk not in the ways of thine heart, and in the sight of thine eyes: but know thou,* **that for all these [things] God will bring thee into judgment** (Eccles. 11:9 [NKJV]).

God has the right to judge us because he made us (Gen. 1:26–7). Homosexual behavior is a sin because God has said it is. In fact, it has been sinful in every period of human existence. It was sinful during the Patriarchal Dispensation (Gen. 18:16–19:29). It was condemned under the Mosaical Dispensation (Lev. 18:22–24). And homosexuality is sinful and condemned under the Christian Dispensation (Rom. 1:26–28). But there is hope for them and all sinners. It's called repentance. The blood of Jesus is available to wash away the sins of all who will repent and turn from their sin. God will forgive all who humbly come to him in faithful obedience.

This is the only message of hope that we have the liberty to extend to those caught up in this errant lifestyle. Over the course of the past thirty years, many people have had their vision blurred by close proximity to homosexuality. They've had family, friends, and coworkers who have embraced homosexuality. Suddenly it is no longer the unnamed stranger; now it's personal. It is someone with whom you have a close connection. What now? What do I do now that it's my son, my niece, my mother, my brother, etc.?

Then one said to him [Jesus], "Look, your mother and your brothers are standing outside, seeking to speak with you." But he answered and said to the one who told him, "Who is my mother and who are my brothers?" And he stretched out his hand toward his disciples and said, "Here are my mother and my brothers! ***For whoever does the will of my Father in heaven is my brother and sister and mother"*** (Matt. 12:48–50 [NKJV]).

And even as they did not like to retain God in their knowledge, God gave them over to a debased mind, to do those things which are not fitting; being filled with all unrighteousness, sexual immorality, wickedness, covetousness, maliciousness; full of envy, murder, strife, deceit, evil-mindedness; they are whisperers, backbiters, haters of God, violent, proud, boasters, inventors of evil things, disobedient to parents, undiscerning, untrustworthy, unloving, unforgiving, unmerciful; who, knowing the righteous judgment of God, that those who practice such things are deserving of death, ***not only do the same but also approve of those who practice them*** (Rom. 1:28–32 [NKJV]).

And have no fellowship *with the unfruitful works of darkness, but rather expose them. For it is shameful even to speak of those things which are done by them in secret* (Eph. 5:11–12 [NKJV]).

Throughout the pages of the Bible, God is very clear: Christians cannot be in full fellowship with him and condone the actions of those living in unrepentant sin. Christians are to live in the world yet not embrace the world to the point of becoming of (like) the world (John 17:14–16). Unfortunately, people of faith have embraced the world to the extent that our country is at a crossroad.

Our choices are to continue on this path to a certain bitter end or embrace the current challenge by preaching, teaching, and exalting the noble purpose of marriage and family. Christians are the protectors and keepers of the marriage covenant. We must enlist, equip, and empower Christian couples to become biblical marriage ambassadors. They must see their marriages as fulfilling the great commission (Matt. 28:18–20). The ball is squarely in our court.

Christians must get off their comfortable couches and pews and go interact with this world. If the current immoral revolution is to be turned around, it is Christians who must do it. We must be the models for a culture where marital fidelity and sexual purity are not only achievable but are the standard that all should ascribe to.

Evil always thrives when righteous people do or say nothing to refute it.

Speak truth freely, while it's still free.

STUDY GUIDE

Chapter 1: Whatever Happened to Free Speech?

The Jewish Holocaust and the African slave trade are but two examples of humans' inhumanity to other humans; are we (humans) capable of such atrocities today? Why or why not?

How might your answer to the previous question make a homosexual feel?

Why are fear and hatred such powerful forces?

What does the following phrase mean: We have seen the enemy and the enemy is us?

Regarding homosexuality, what impact does current public opinion have on freedom of speech?

In your opinion, is America strong enough to withstand hate speech and love speech?

What was the consensus public opinion in America seventy-five years ago regarding homosexuality? How did this impact the way homosexuals were treated publicly?

What caused the changes that we see today? What role has our silence played?

What is God's view of homosexuality (Lev. 18:22, Rom. 1:26–8)?

In spite of scripture (Matt. 12:48–50, Eph. 5:11–12, Rom 1:28–32), why do you think some people change their views when their friend, son or daughter embraces the homosexual lifestyle?

Since creation has God's view ever been different? Scripturally defend your position (Patriarchal Dispensation, Mosaical Dispensation, Christian Dispensation)?

What is Political Correctness (PC)?

(The next 2 questions are intended to be rhetorical; for your personal introspection only) How PC are you when you aren't around Christians? Considering your lifestyle how *of the world* are you?

In what ways may someone use his or her marriage to fulfill the great commission?

When does the book say that evil thrives? Explain why you agree for disagree.

Personal take away:

_____

_____

_____

Chapter 2
HOMOPHOBIA

Those who don't know history are doomed to repeat it. — Edmund Burke

That which has been is what will be, that which is done is what will be done, And there is nothing new under the sun. (Eccles. 1:9 [NKJV])

I am going to venture a guess that for many of us world history was not our favorite subject. Generally human beings do not fully appreciate history until they have lived through events that are being studied in current history books. With these thoughts in mind, the following review of world history is included to help everyone fully appreciate the historical narrative that *homophobia* fits into.

The word **propaganda** comes from the Vatican. The phrase *congregatio de propaganda fide* (the congregation for the propagation of the faith) was used to support the catholic faith in response to the Protestant Reformation. Propaganda is everywhere and has been around for a very long time. Every newspaper, magazine, news channel, radio station, advertisement, or any other type of mass media contains elements of propaganda. Propaganda is often given a negative connotation due to its history of power and control.

According to *Webster's College Dictionary*, propaganda is "information or ideas methodically spread to promote or to injure a cause, movement, nation etc. and the deliberate spread of such information or ideas." Whether the reader of a media source agrees or disagrees with the content, the purpose of the media is to convey only one way to look at a particular situation or idea.

One of the most well-known propaganda experts in war history was Adolf Hitler. Hitler's use of war propaganda resulted in convincing his country of the National Socialism ideals, which ultimately resulted in the Holocaust and the extermination of millions of Jewish people. Hitler's use of propaganda in spreading his beliefs of National Socialism and his dislike of the Jews resulted in the support of his army and country and the outbreak of World War II.

In the same fashion as Hitler, during World War II (1939–45) American propaganda was used to increase support for the war and commitment to an Allied victory. Using a vast array of media, propagandists stirred up hatred for the enemy and support for America's allies, urged greater public effort for war production and victory gardens, persuaded people to save some of their material so that more material could be used for the war effort, and sold war bonds.

Patriotism became the central theme of advertising throughout the war, as large scale campaigns were launched to sell war bonds, promote efficiency in factories, reduce ugly rumors, and maintain civilian morale. The war consolidated the advertising industry's role in American society, deflecting earlier criticism.

As in Britain, American propaganda depicted the war as an issue of good versus evil, which allowed the government to encourage its population to fight a "just war," and used themes of resistance in, and liberation to, the occupied countries. In 1940, even prior to being drawn into World War II, President Roosevelt urged every American to consider the effect if the dictatorships won in Europe and Asia.

Precision bombing was praised, exaggerating its accuracy, to convince people of the difference between good and bad bombing. Hitler, Tojo, Mussolini, and their followers were the villains in American film, even in cartoons where characters, such as Bugs Bunny, would defeat them—a practice that began before Pearl Harbor. Cartoons depicted Axis leaders as not being human: Germany (Hitler), Italy (Mussolini), Japan (Hirohito), and others.

The Office of War Information suggested plot lines using Axis agents in place of traditional villainous roles, such as the rustler in Westerns. Hitler was often depicted in situations ridiculing him, and editorial cartoons usually depicted him in caricature. Hitler's dictatorship was often heavily satirized. To raise morale, even prior to the turning of the war in the Allies favor, Hitler often appeared in editorial cartoons as doomed. He and the German people were depicted as fools.

For example, in an editorial cartoon by Dr. Seuss, a German father scolded his hungry son, telling him that the Germans ate countries, not food. All Germans were often stereotyped as evil in films and posters, although many atrocities were specifically ascribed to Nazis and Hitler specifically, rather than to the German people.

In anti-Italian propaganda Mussolini appeared in situations ridiculing him. Editorial cartoons depicted him as a two-bit dictator. Italians were often stereotyped as evil in films and posters. Propaganda portrayed the Japanese as a foreign, grotesque and uncivilized enemy. American propagandists portrayed the Japanese as blindly fanatic and ruthless, with a history of desiring overseas conquests. Atrocities were ascribed to the Japanese people as a whole. Even Japanese-Americans would be portrayed as massively supporting Japan, only awaiting the signal to commit sabotage.

As a result of propaganda, 110,000 people of Japanese heritage who lived on the Pacific coast of the United States were forced into internment camps. The US government ordered their internment in 1942 shortly after Imperial Japan's attack on Pearl Harbor. President Franklin D. Roosevelt authorized the internment with Executive Order 9066, issued February 19, 1942, which allowed local military commanders to designate "military areas" as "exclusion zones," from which "any or all persons may be excluded." This power was used to declare that all people of Japanese ancestry were excluded from the entire Pacific coast, including all of California and much of Oregon, Washington, and Arizona, except for those in internment camps.

As stated in the opening, propaganda is everywhere and has been around for a long time. Be it wartime or peacetime, someone is always launching an assault to influence or control the minds of the masses. A key tactic in this assault is an attempt to define oneself and to define or redefine the opposition. In psychology and sociology, identity is a person's conception and expression of their individuality or group affiliations. Identity may be further defined as the distinctive characteristic belonging to any given individual, or shared by members of a particular social category or group. *Sexual orientation identity* describes how persons identify their own sexualities. Arriving at this identity greatly affects one's mental model of oneself. This decision has a great psychological impact and determines a person's self-image and self-esteem.

Throughout human history homosexuality was, more often than not, considered an unnatural act, and thereby those who participated in such acts were shunned by society. In fact, in many instances they were put to death. *Propaganda* and social stigmas were used to reinforce the dominate position that all forms of homosexual behavior is an abomination. However, the last thirty years have brought about a drastic change in public acceptance of what is now defined as the LGBT community.

Beginning in the 1970s propaganda has been utilized to influence or change the public's view about homosexuality. In the last generation it has been used to define homosexuals as a distinct group or class suffering under the weight of second-class citizenship. Their advocates put forth the assertion that homosexuality is a condition imposed at birth. And for a people or a government to deny or limit their rights to full and free expression of their natural homosexual nature is to deny them the very essence of their *identity*.

Therefore, the United States of America must put off the archaic notions of a midevil age and fully live up to its immortal declaration that all men are created equal and that they are endowed by their creator with certain unalienable rights, that among these are life, liberty and the pursuit of happiness. As you have just read, propaganda can be eloquently stated.

This represented a rare moment in human history when a group of people chose to define their identity by a certain behavior. To be sure, as designed by God, our sexual nature is a significant part of our identity. However our sexual identity is not the sum total of who we are. In the current moral revolution, some people have replaced their biological identity (as designed by God) with a social identity (as chosen by the individual).

In today's culture a person in search of sexual fulfillment is whatever he or she *thinks* him or her self to be. If a person is unable to reconcile their biological identity with their social identity, maybe sex has become an idol. If so, they will always, erroneously, believe that a lack of sexual fulfillment is a lack of human fulfillment.

If the first wave of propaganda was defensive, the second wave is definitely offensive. For much of the twentieth century, homosexuality was defined by the medical and scientific community as a psychiatric disorder. In the last several decades, however, "homosexuality" has been removed from the diagnostic manual of mental disorders, and the research emphasis has shifted to the other side of the equation: the study of the negative, sometimes pathological reactions to homosexuals by heterosexuals. In essence, if homosexuals are normal, then there must be something abnormal about those who oppose or harbor ill will against them.

The term "homophobia" has gained currency as a one-word summary of this widespread "problem." The root of the term "homophobia," which was coined by George Weinberg, a psychologist, in the 1960s, means "fear" or "morbid fear." Weinberg describes the concept as a medical phobia. *Merriam Webster Dictionary:* irrational fear of, aversion to, or discrimination against homosexuality or homosexuals; unreasoning fear of or antipathy toward homosexuals and homosexuality; *Random House Dictionary:* intense hatred or fear of homosexuals or homosexuality.

Labeling anti-LGBT prejudice as a social problem worthy of scholarly attention was not new. A 1969 article in *Time* magazine described examples of negative attitudes toward homosexuality as "homophobia" including "a mixture of revulsion and apprehension" which some called homosexual panic. In 1971, Kenneth Smith used homophobia as a personality profile to describe the psychological aversion to homosexuality. Weinberg also used it this way in his 1972 book *Society and the Healthy Homosexual*, published one year before the American Psychiatric Association voted to remove homosexuality from its list of mental disorders. Weinberg's term became an important tool for gay and lesbian activists, advocates, and their allies.

A *phobia* is, when used in the context of clinical psychology, a type of anxiety disorder, usually defined as a persistent fear of an object or situation in which the sufferer commits to great lengths in avoiding, typically disproportional to the actual danger posed, often being recognized as *irrational*. In the event the phobia cannot be avoided entirely, the sufferer will endure the situation or object with marked distress and significant interference in social or occupational activities.

Homophobia has never been listed as part of a clinical taxonomy of phobias, neither in the Diagnostic and Statistical Manual of Mental Disorders (DSM) or International Statistical Classification of Diseases and Related Health Problems (ICD).

In 1973 The American Psychiatric Association (APA), recognizing the power of the stigma against homosexuality, issued the following statement, reaffirmed by the Board of Trustees, July 2011: "Whereas homosexuality per se implies no impairment in judgment, stability, reliability, or general social or vocational capabilities, the APA calls on all international health organizations, psychiatric organizations, and individual psychiatrists in other countries to urge the repeal in their own countries of legislation that penalizes homosexual acts by consenting adults in private. Further, APA calls on these organizations and individuals to do all that is possible to decrease the stigma related to homosexuality wherever and whenever it may occur."

Since the early 1980s, scientists attempting to measure homophobia have developed a number of different homophobia scales and questionnaires. In 1996, as part of his study on homophobia, Dr. Henry Adams and his colleagues at the University of Georgia developed their own "Homophobia Scale" by modifying scales used by other researchers in earlier studies. It's a twenty-five-item questionnaire "designed to measure your thoughts, feelings and behaviors with regards to homosexuality." The instructions stressed: "It is not a test, so there is no right or wrong answers."

If homophobia is a mental malady, it follows that there must of necessity be a treatment plan for it. The list below includes some of the treatments for homophobia mentioned in various sources (They state that one should always seek professional medical advice about any treatment or change in treatment plans):

- Behavior therapy, antianxiety medication
- Psychotherapy
- Cognitive-behavioral therapy (CBT)
- Exposure therapy
- Relaxation techniques—controlled breathing, visualization
- Medication
- Medications to treat anxiety may be utilized, but there are no studies that support the efficacy of medication in the treatment of specific phobias.

Again, **propaganda** is *information or ideas methodically spread to promote or to injure a cause, movement, nation etc. and the deliberate spread of such information or ideas.*

This document is intended for those who believe the Bible, disagree with homosexuality, and thus are labeled as suffering from homophobia. Be of good courage, as of this writing (2014) this is not a medical malady, possibly the term was created to serve as retribution for the years that homosexuals languished under the designation of "mental illness." Presently those advocating for homosexuality have the upper hand. Their propaganda is winning the day.

If you are still not at ease embracing the "homophobic" moniker, consider what God said about homosexuality: *You shall not lie with a male as with a woman. It is an abomination* (Lev. 18:22 [NKJV]). Such a positon makes God the first person deserving of the homophobic label. If you're standing with God this puts you in pretty lofty company. All Christians should be quite at ease whenever someone find any correlation between God and him or her.

Good people, we have been silent for far too long: the time has now well past; you must speak now. When you do speak, speak truth, speak love, speak with integrity; speak words that unequivocally condemn the darkness of homosexuality while simultaneously reaffirm that the person is *fearfully and wonderfully made* (Ps. 139:14 [NKJV]).

Speak truth freely, while it's still free!

STUDY GUIDE

Chapter 2: Homophobia

What is the definition of propaganda?

Who invented propaganda and for what purpose?

How was propaganda used in World War II?

Describe the first wave of propaganda to influence or change the public's view about homosexuality.

Prior to 1973 how was homosexuality defined by the American Psychiatric Association?

Since 1973 how has propaganda been used by homosexual advocates to redefine their identity?

What are some of the outcomes when a person believes their sexual identity is the sum total of who they are as a person?

Explain how propaganda has been used to silence heterosexuals who disagree with homosexuality.

Medically what is a phobia?

Is homophobia a phobia? Why or why not?

Who is the first person deserving of the homophobic label? Support your answer with scripture.

Are all homosexuals fearfully and wonderfully made? Defend your position with scripture. How does this impact your treatment of them?

Personal take away:

_____

_____

_____

Chapter 3
SEXUAL ORIENTATION

Given that man is made in the image of God, humans are the only species on the planet with the ability to imagine and to contemplate. These abilities have been the driving force behind humanity's quest *to boldly go where no one has ever gone before.* Throughout history humans have been in search of some new thing. In the book of Acts, some men, with too much time on their hand, busily put their ability to imagine and contemplate to unprofitable use:

Now while Paul waited for them at Athens, his spirit was provoked within him when he saw that the city was given over to idols. Therefore he reasoned in the synagogue with the Jews and with the Gentile worshipers, and in the marketplace daily with those who happened to be there. Then certain Epicurean and Stoic philosophers encountered him. And some said, "What does this babbler want to say?" Others said, "He seems to be a proclaimer of foreign gods," because he preached to them Jesus and the resurrection.

And they took him and brought him to the Areopagus, saying, "May we know what this new doctrine is of which you speak? For you are bringing some strange things to our ears. Therefore we want to know what these things mean." For all the Athenians and the foreigners who were there **spent their time in nothing else but either to tell or to hear some new thing.**

Then Paul stood in the midst of the Areopagus and said, "Men of Athens, I perceive that in all things you are very religious; for as I was passing through and considering the objects of your worship, I even found an altar with this inscription:
'TO THE UNKNOWN GOD" (Acts 17:19–23a [NKJV]).

Like the Athenians, today mankind is still in search of some new thing. In fact modern man has surpassed the Athenians, Corinthians, and the Romans in pursuit of sexual immorality. Homosesual advocates have sought to legitimize their illicit desires by redefining mankind's sexual nature: *Sexual orientation is an enduring personal quality that inclines people to feel romantic or sexual attraction (or a combination of these) to persons of the opposite sex or gender, the same sex or gender, or to both sexes or more than one gender.*

In the past several decades sexual orientation has been the corner stone of a carefully crafted propaganda campaign to bring ligitimacy to the homosexual lifestyle. From the early 1900s through the 1960s, psychological research revealed that compared to the general public, homosexuals exhibited higher levels of depression and psychological maladies. Many of the researchers concluded that the elevated levels of depression in the homosexual community were directly attributable to the weight of the social stigma placed upon them and not to any mental deficiency.

In the end, unsurprisingly, their premise was confirmed: the stigmatization of homosexuality causes mental stress in the minds of those who practice it; furthermore, homosexuality is *a normal variation of human sexual orientation.* In 1973 these findings were used to persuade the American Psychiatric Association to remove homosexuality from their list of mental illnesses. And from this point forward, homosexual advocates have been on a mission to gain full public acceptance including their ability to freely and openly express the homosexual lifestyle in whatsoever manner they choose.

Sexual Orientation

With the stigma of mental illness removed, the advocates only needed to validate how one arrives at the condition of being homosexual. And there you have it: sexual orientation; at once this term, for millions of people removed the stigma of sin and gave them free and open access to the pursuit of their passions. It's amazing what humans can do with a little *imagination and contemplation.*

Every year in America millions of toddlers are burned by touching fire or something hot. If we were to commission a research study, would our focus be to discover a way for a toddler to touch fire and not get burned or to train toddlers not to touch fire? Obviously we'd choose the latter. The reality is, as every parent knows, even a toddler is capable of learning and obeying the natural laws of the universe: **fire, hot, burn hurts, don't touch**. Apparently, homosexual advocates would have us believe humans lose this ability to exhibit such self-control after age three.

Paul Joseph Goebbels (October 29, 1897–May 1, 1945) was Adolf Hitler's Propaganda Minister in Nazi Germany. He also served as chancellor for one day, following Hitler's death. He was known for his zealous and energetic oratory and intense anti-Semitism. Following is an excerpt from a speech by Goebbels on January 9, 1928 to an audience of party members for a series of training talks for Nazi party members in Berlin:

"To attract people, to win over people to that which I have realized as being true, that is called propaganda. In the beginning there is the understanding, this understanding uses propaganda as a tool to find those men that shall turn understanding into politics. Success is the important thing. Propaganda is not a matter for average minds, but rather a matter for practitioners. It is not supposed to be lovely or theoretically correct. I do not care if I give wonderful, aesthetically elegant speeches, or speak so that women cry. The point of a political speech is to persuade people of what we think right."

Following is an excerpt from "Aus Churchill's Lügenfabrik" ("Churchill's Lie Factory"), January 12, 1941, *Die Zeit ohne Beispiel* (Munich: Zentralverlag der NSDAP, 1941), pp. 364–369: "That is of course rather painful for those involved. One should not as a rule, reveal one's secrets, since one does not know if and when one may need them again. The essential English leadership secret does not depend on particular intelligence. Rather, it depends on a remarkably stupid thick-headedness. The English follow the principle that when one lies, one should lie big, and stick to it. They keep up their lies, even at the risk of looking *ridiculous*."

Although the following quote is attributed to Goebbels, the fact that it cannot be substantiated doesn't diminish its truthfulness and its ability to stand on its own. In essence, he is reported to have said: *If you repeat a lie often enough, people will believe it, and you will even come to believe it yourself.*

The coming of the lawless one is according to the working of Satan, with all power, signs, and lying wonders and with all unrighteous deception among those who perish, because they did not receive the love of the truth, that they might be saved. And for this reason **God will send them strong delusions that they should believe the lie** *that they all may be condemned who did not believe the truth but had pleasure in unrighteousness* (2 Thess. 2:9–12 [NKJV]).

The curious thing about humans and lying is, as stated above, many will indeed hold to the lie even at the risk of looking and sounding ridiculous. They will sound ridiculous because from the start, they set out to *defend an indefensible position*. Let's consider just how ridiculous the concept of sexual orientation is. The first challenge one has when one sets out to defend an unnatural position is that they cannot use known words correctly. They are left with the desperate options of changing the meaning of existing words or making up new words.

Again, their definition of sexual orientation: "Sexual orientation is an enduring personal quality that inclines people to feel romantic or sexual attraction (or a combination of these) to persons of the opposite sex or gender, the same sex or gender, or to both sexes or more than one gender."

Based on *the Random House Dictionary*: **Orientation** (noun): the act or process of orienting or the state of being oriented.

The root word **orient** (verb used with object):

1. to adjust with relation to, or bring into due relation to surroundings, circumstances, facts, etc.
2. to direct or position toward a particular object: *Orient it toward that house.*
3. to determine the position of in relation to the points of the compass; get the bearings of.

It has been said, "The person who controls the language, controls the debate." By controlling ideas, you can control the way people think and act. Nowhere has this been more evident than in the culture war over the issue of *human sexuality*. In an attempt to steer the debate and further their cause, proponents of the social acceptance of homosexuality have sought to redefine the American vocabulary and impose new terminology that casts sinful behavior in a favorable light.

At the same time, our historical understanding of many words is being challenged through societal pressure to conform to a "politically correct" philosophical agenda. The term "sexual orientation disturbance" was coined in 1973 when the American Psychological Association (APA) debated removing homosexuality from its list of sexual disorders. Sometime after this, the word "disturbance" was dropped, and professionals and experts adopted the phrase "sexual orientation."

Activists interested in promoting the idea that an individual's sexual attractions were closely related to heredity, or a so-called "gay gene," capitalized on the opportunity. If a person's sexual attractions are part of their "orientation," or genetic makeup, the thought goes, then those attractions must be completely natural and acceptable, regardless of whom the subject of those attractions may be.

Although most members of the scientific community agree there is no legitimate scientific basis for such a claim, this notion has been effectively promoted and marketed, hence the widespread acceptance of the lie of "sexual orientation." Interestingly, "sexual orientation" was preceded by "sexual preference"—a term that fell out of favor around the mid-1980s. One must admit that "orientation" has a scientific ring to it that "preference" lacks, and this helped cement the idea into societal use. "Preference" is more casual, similar to preferring corn over carrots, while "orientation" suggests something less subjective; something more "hardwired" into an individual.

Homosexual activists have seized control of the language and they continue to market their terminology to the public through their allies in the media, government and mental health institutions. Concerned citizens must learn to recognize the use of lies such as "sexual orientation" and resist the pressure to compromise the truth about human sexuality. God made Adam and Eve "fit" for one another; he made them male and female, no additional "*orientation*" necessary or assembly required.

In the *Wizard of Oz,* Dorothy's dog Toto pulls back the curtain to reveal the wizard pulling levers to produce the scary scene of fire and smoke. When he realizes they could see him, in a last ditch effort to keep the charade going, he exclaims, **Pay no attention to the man behind the curtain!** Homosexual advocates would have us, *Pay no attention to the real meaning of the word orientation!* In essence they are suggesting we all pretend to be insane together for a while.

Sexual Orientation

And the Lord God caused a deep sleep to fall on Adam, and he slept; and He took one of his ribs, and closed up the flesh in its place. Then the rib which the Lord God had taken from man He made into a woman, and He brought her to the man.

*And Adam said, "This is now bone of my bones and flesh of my flesh; She shall be called woman, because she was taken out of man." Therefore, a man shall leave his father and mother and be joined to his wife, and they shall become one flesh. And they were both naked, **the man and his wife**, and were not ashamed. (Genesis 2:21–25 [NKJV]).*

The lie of sexual orientation is mutually exclusive from, and wholly contradictory to, God's design of humanity. Definition number one above for "orient" is *to adjust with relation to, or bring into due relation to, surroundings, circumstances, facts, etc.* Homosexual advocates are not intellectually honest; therein is the road they travel to sounding ridiculous. If they were honest, their position would be, 'We have chosen to orient ourselves to pursue our passions, rather than exercise self-control and live according to God's natural design.' Throughout human history, in an effort to defend their position, humans have often sought to *turn the truth of God into a lie* (Rom. 1:24–26 [NKJV]).

And yet today human's feeble attempts to do so are continuing. In the foreword you read the edits made to scriptures that clearly condemn the practice of homosexuality. They say, "The Bible can be interpreted in different ways, leading to what we call *interpretive ambiguity*." Therefore, "The Queen James Bible seeks to resolve interpretive ambiguity in the Bible as it pertains to homosexuality: We (the publisher) edited those eight verses in a way that makes homophobic interpretations impossible."

Below are the unedited versions of the passages where those verses are taken from:

Sodom's Depravity

Now the two angels came to Sodom in the evening, and Lot was sitting in the gate of Sodom. When Lot saw them, he rose to meet them, and he bowed himself with his face toward the ground. And he said, "Here now, my lords, please turn in to your servant's house and spend the night, and wash your feet; then you may rise early and go on your way." And they said, "No, but we will spend the night in the open square."

But he insisted strongly; so they turned in to him and entered his house. Then he made them a feast, and baked unleavened bread, and they ate. Now before they lay down, the men of the city, the men of Sodom, both old and young, all the people from every quarter, surrounded the house. And they called to Lot and said to him, "Where are the men who came to you tonight? Bring them out to us that we may know them carnally."

So Lot went out to them through the doorway, shut the door behind him, and said, "Please, my brethren, do not do so wickedly! See now, I have two daughters who have not known a man; please, let me bring them out to you, and you may do to them as you wish; only do nothing to these men, since this is the reason they have come under the shadow of my roof."

And they said, "Stand back!" Then they said, "This one came in to stay here, and he keeps acting as a judge; now we will deal worse with you than with them." So they pressed hard against the man Lot and came near to breaking down the door. But the men reached out their hands and pulled Lot into the house with them, and shut the door. And they struck the men who were at the doorway of the house with blindness, both small and great, so that they became weary trying to find the door (Genesis 19:1–11 [NKJV]).

Abomination (Hebrew and Greek): to be offensive morally; (make to) be abhorred, something disgusting (morally), that is, (as noun) an abhorrence, a detestation (*From Strongs Hebrew & Greek Dictionary*)

You shall not lie with a male as with a woman. It is an abomination (Lev. 18:22 [NKJV]).

If a man lies with a male as he lies with a woman, both of them have committed an abomination. They shall surely be put to death. Their blood shall be upon them (Lev. 20:13 [NKJV]).

Vile Passions

For this reason God gave them up to vile passions. For even their women exchanged the natural use for what is against nature. Likewise also the men, leaving the natural use of the woman, burned in their lust for one another, men with men committing what is shameful, and receiving in themselves the penalty of their error which was due.

And even as they did not like to retain God in their knowledge, God gave them over to a debased mind, to do those things which are not fitting; being filled with all unrighteousness, sexual immorality…who, knowing the righteous judgment of God, that those who practice such things are deserving of death, not only do the same but also approve of those who practice them (Rom. 1:26–29a, 32 [NKJV]).

The Unrighteous

Do you not know that the unrighteous will not inherit the kingdom of God? Do not be deceived. Neither fornicators, nor idolaters, nor adulterers, nor homosexuals, nor sodomites, nor thieves, nor covetous, nor drunkards, nor revilers, nor extortioners will inherit the kingdom of God.

And such were some of you. But you were washed, but you were sanctified, but you were justified in the name of the Lord Jesus and by the Spirit of our God (1 Cor. 6:9–11 [NKJV]).

Law Is for Law Breakers

But we know that the law is good if one uses it lawfully, knowing this: that the law is not made for a righteous person, but for the lawless and insubordinate, for the ungodly and for sinners, for the unholy and profane, for murderers of fathers and murderers of mothers, for manslayers, for fornicators, **for sodomites,** *for kidnappers, for liars, for perjurers, and if there is any other thing that is contrary to sound doctrine, according to the glorious gospel of the blessed God which was committed to my trust* (1 Tim. 1:8–11 [NKJV]).

Judgment

But I want to remind you, though you once knew this, that the Lord, having saved the people out of the land of Egypt, afterward destroyed those who did not believe. And the angels who did not keep their proper domain, but left their own abode, He has reserved in everlasting chains under darkness for the judgment of the great day; as Sodom and Gomorrah, and the cities around them in a similar manner to these, having **given themselves over to sexual immorality and gone after strange flesh***, are set forth as an example, suffering the vengeance of eternal fire* (Jude 1:5–7 [NKJV]).

In Genesis 3:8 Adam and Eve, after eating the forbidden fruit, try to hide from God. How ridiculous is that? Yes, but is it more ridiculous than changing God's Word to live out your vile passions with a clear conscience? One will always look and sound ridiculous when one tries to justify any stance one takes that's contrary to the Word of God. God said Eve was **"fit"** or compatible for Adam. Why on earth would any man or woman ever need to be **"oriented"** in order to become sexually compatible with another human being? This orientation would only be required to make them compatible for someone of the same gender.

Sexual Orientation

They, homosexuals, claim that their "sexual orientation" is a result of their natural genetic makeup and provides the only opportunity for them to live in an intimate loving relationship. In the face of someone who makes such an assertion, as lovingly as you can, you may simply reply: *ridiculous.*

Social stigmas are a natural way that civilizations discourage deviant behavior. This is true even when the stigmatized behavior is something that God would allow, but society chooses to reject. Societal norms don't just pop up out of thin air. **Certainly it is not always the case**, but oftentimes normalized human behavior is rooted in God's design.

There is a reason why we don't randomly slap people upside the head just because we felt like it or tell a lie every time the truth would be uncomfortable or unprofitable. The normalized behaviors of keeping our hands to ourselves and telling the truth are rooted in our design. God knew that humanity could not live in peace and harmony if people were free to relate openly to each other in this manner.

Therefore, he forbade us from physically assaulting one another: *Whoever sheds man's blood, By man his blood shall be shed; For in the image of God He made man* (Gen. 9:6–7 [NKJV]). He also forbade us from lying to each other: *A false witness will not go unpunished, and he who speaks lies shall perish* (Prov. 19:9 [NKJV]).

Yes, we are free to do both, but these activities put strain on human relationships and cause much anxiety and stress in those who regularly practice such behavior. Over the course of time, there are shifts and modifications in normalized behaviors. However, *behavior that is intrinsic to the stability and sustainability of the species remains all but constant,* absent unnatural stimuli that eminates from humans' unrestrained imagination and contemplation. God created Adam oriented for Eve: no further orientation required.

Geese are but Geese tho' we may think them Swans; and Truth will be Truth tho' it sometimes proves mortifying and distasteful.   Benjamin Franklin

Speak truth freely, while it's still free.

STUDY GUIDE

Chapter 3: Sexual Orientation

Name some of the beneficial outcomes of humans' ability to imagine and to contemplate? (Hint: electricity)

In the book of Acts what was the outcome when men contemplated God?

What is the generally accepted definition of sexual orientation?

When and why was homosexuality removed from the American Psychiatric Association's (APA) list of mental illness?

As a result of the APA's decision, what has been the mission of homosexual activists?

Who was Paul Joseph Goebbels, and what were some of his philosophies?

What is the correlation between Goebbels's quote on lying and 2 Thessalonians 2:9–12?

As it relates to using words, what options does one have when one tries to defend an indefensible position?

What is the definition of the word orientation?

"He or she who controls the language, controls the debate." Do you agree or disagree?

Why do you think the word "disturbance" was dropped from the original term: "sexual orientation disturbance?"

How did homosexual advocates use "orientation" to support "genetic makeup?"

Why did "sexual orientation" win out over "sexual preference?"

What did God mean when He said Eve was fit for Adam?

If homosexual advocates were intellectually honest, what would their stance be?

What are some harms and benefits of social norms?

Personal take away:

_____

_____

_____

Chapter 4
A MOTHER'S LOVE

No one will ever love you like your mother loves you.

A mom's hug lasts long after she lets go.

A mother's love is patient and forgiving when all others are forsaking.

A mother is one you can always count on…who loves you no matter what…who is there for you whenever you need her and never lets you down.

No language can express the power, beauty, and heroism of a mother's love.

A mother's love has no expiration date.

"Grown" means nothing to a mother. A child is a child. They get older and bigger, but grown? In a mother's heart each will always be her baby.

The purest and truest meaning of the word "unconditional" can only be found in a mother's love.

The sweetest sounds to mortals given are heard in mother, home, and heaven.

Before you were conceived, I wanted you. Before you were born, I loved you. Before you were here an hour, I would have died for you.

All this and more is a mother's love.

Mothers know something fathers cannot and will not ever know. They know what it feels like to conceive, develop, and deliver a new life form into this world. They are the only ones on the planet who know what creating life actually feels like. Therefore, who can deny that a mother and her child share an exclusively special bond that no one else on earth can know?

This is not to say that fathers do not or cannot love their children **deeply**. As a point fact, fathers do play a *costarring role* in the life creation process. Fathers love differently. It is unrealistic to expect fathers to love LIKE mothers because fathers are different physically, psychologically, emotionally, etc.

It is assumed that if you are reading this material, someone has already had the birds-and-bees discussion with you. It is presumed you understand that there is a great inequity in the amount of time each parent is personally engaged in the creation process. A father's intimate and direct participation is concluded at the end of one romantic evening, while a mother **labors** for the next forty-two weeks.

No father has ever felt the pangs of an unborn child kicking him in his ribs. As a result of this and many other experiences only mothers can have, it is universally accepted that mothers have a uniquely special bond with their children. This is in no way a knock against fathers. God's design requires both to create a child, and it takes both to raise and nurture him/her in the manner in which he intended. A father's love, guidance, and discipline are crucial to shaping and molding children into the people God created them to be. Were it not so, God could have made procreation a solo act.

In our American culture, mothers are typically the ones entrusted with the daily nurturing and caregiving of our children. Every mother knows the joy of bathing and dressing her infant child. She lays out the clothes she's going to dress her baby in, draws the water (and tests it to make sure it's not too hot), and then patiently and tenderly bathes her precious little bundle of joy. She removes her baby from the water, towel dries him or her, and then gently massages his or her little body with *Johnson's Baby Oil*. Many mothers have gone, and many more will go to their graves with memories of bath time and the smell of *Johnson's Baby Oil* permanently implanted deeply within their subconscious.

The first birthday comes so quickly—has it been a year already? Family and friends come from near and far to celebrate *year 1* in the life of her precious little _____ (insert your favorite nickname here). Before the mother knows it, she's smack dab in the middle of the terrible two's, and then year three is a distant blur, and she now finds herself standing on the steps of a pre-K schoolhouse. Somehow through the mental fog, she can make out that the teacher is telling her that she must leave now.

"Leave? You want me to leave?" The mother thinks: "You mean leave without my precious little _____ (insert your favorite nickname here)? You don't understand: counting the gestational period I have been solely responsible for this child for the past 1,740 days. And now on day 1,741, you want me to just turn around and leave him alone here, with you?" Somehow, without the aid of security, she does manage to walk out of the building and make it back to her car. She sits in a blind stupor for a few moments before gaining enough composure and mental clarity to start the car and safely drive away.

The years and milestones come and go: birthdays, sleepovers, camping trips, T-ball, Little League, etc. One weekend morning she's downstairs in the kitchen cooking breakfast. Her son comes up behind her and says excitedly, "Mom, turn around!" Wondering what's going on, she briskly twirls around. He walks right up to her face and jubilantly shouts, "Mom! I am taller than you!" This isn't her first rodeo; long before now she learned that boys are all about conquest. So she gives him a BIG congratulatory hug and relishes his latest conquest with him. She bites her lip as he walks away and exclaims, "You will be looking up to me *for the rest of your life!*"

For the next few years, his social peer group becomes the center of his world. The mother and son don't have the long walks and talks that they used to. She does notice some changes in him and is aware of the growing emotional distance between the two of them. She still longs for the closeness they once had, and she wants him to share everything that's going on his world with her. She resists the urge to pry because he's a high school senior now and she only has one more year with him at home. She gives him his space and allows him to decide the type of person that he is going to be when he leaves home.

In the blink of an eye, she's sitting in an auditorium, dressed in her Sunday best, where hundreds of wide-eyed eighteen year olds have donned caps and gowns. As she sits there in a foggy daze, her mind wanders back and forth from this moment to one of the millions of moments that have occurred over the past eighteen years. In the distance she can make out that a voice is sounding out syllables that appear to be first, middle, and last names. Then suddenly she hears a sequence that her brain recognizes as an alternate identifier for her precious little _____ (insert your favorite nickname here).

The next morning she arises from a night of restlessness, goes downstairs, and gets a cup of coffee or tea to regain full consciousness. She's waiting to hear sounds from his room that he has awakened from his slumber. She goes into his room and sits on his bed. She caresses his hand and looks into his tender young eyes. Inside she's summoning all the composure she can to resist bawling her eyes out.

Her initial impulse is to refer to him as _____ (insert your favorite nickname here); however, sensing this is a moment of transition from boyhood to manhood, she calls him by his big boy name: "____, I have loved you with all my heart since the day you were conceived. Every joy that you've had for the past eighteen years has been my joy. Every hurt that you have endured has been my hurt. At the end of the summer, you will leave me and venture out into the world. Out there you will encounter more joys and more hurts; although you will not share all of them with me, I will feel them. I want you to know that there is nothing you can do to close the door of my heart to you. I love you, and I will always be here for you."

He reaches out and gives her a big hug, and he whispers, "I love you, too, Mom. **PS**—*you'll still be looking up to me for the rest of your life.*"

The summer has flown by and the day of departure to college has arrived. All his things are packed, and the famiy is ready to drive him to the next phase of his life. As the car is leaving the driveway, his mother wants to stop, throw it in reverse, and go back and relive these eighteen years again. All along the drive, she vacillates between the panic of turning the car around and the calm of, "I am all right; it is time."

The first year was hard, but with each month and each phone call from him, it got better. She could hear the changes in his voice and tone. Although he wasn't sharing much information about his personal relationships, she could tell that he had found a peer group where he fit and that he was comfortable. In year two she could definitely hear and see that he was a changed person and that he no longer regarded himself as her precious little _____ (insert your favorite nickname here). He talked differently, and the things he talked about were different. In the back of her mind, she began to have thoughts that she would not allow herself to contemplate. She told herself, this is silly, this is ridiculous; I banish these stupid thoughts from my mind.

During the holiday break of his sophomore or junior year, the extended family has gathered at her house to celebrate the holidays. The house is decorated just the way she likes it, and everyone has pitched in to prepare the food. The family patriarch gives the customary gratitude for the food and for the bounty that has been bestowed upon one and all. After dinner the young kids have scurried down to the basement and are playing video games; upstairs some have cleared the dining room table, and they're engaged in a spirited card game, while others are milling about in the den watching sports.

Her son grabs her by the hand and says, "Hey, Mom, let's go to my room; I want to talk to you." Inside his mother is thinking as she goes up the stairs, "This boy hasn't wanted to talk to me in the past three years; every piece of information I have I've had to pry out of him." They go into the room, close the door, and she sits on his bed as he stands. He's twirling his fingers nervously as he begins to speak, "Mom, I..." He stops, walks over to the window, and peers out into the yard.

He slowly turns around to face his mother and continues: "Mom, I love you dearly, and I'm so appreciative for all that you've done for me. I have never wanted to hurt you or to disappoint you. But Mom, I have changed; I am no longer that little boy that you raised. I am a man now, and I have made some decisions about how I want to live my life. *Mom, I am gay.*"

At that moment, for her, the earth stopped rotating on its axis. It was one of those moments when she thought she heard someone say something that was unfathomable to her; her whole being refused to perceive it. Her ears refused to hear it, her brain refused to process it, and her central nervous system refused to respond to it. However, as we often do in those deja vu moments, she involuntarily asked her son to repeat what he just said. And he again said, "Mom, I am gay."

He continued, "And I want to tell the family right now." At this moment his mother becomes paralyzed. Her body is void of emotion and physical sensation. Although her eyes are open, her brain does not recognize the physical mass of humanity before her. Although her son continues to speak, she does not comprehend one word. Involuntarily, she grabs his pillow from the bed and lies in the fetal position. He stops speaking and turns to walk downstairs where he addresses the family.

Six months later the mother awakens in a cold sweat in the middle of the night, and her life begins again at that moment. She has vague memories of countless conversations with friends and family trying to console her. Some tried to do so by imploring that all that matters is he's happy now. If this is the lifestyle that makes him happy, if she still loves him, she will embrace him and his partner and be happy for them.

Of the millions of scenarios that she had imagined for his life, this is not one of them. His lifestyle choice has wrecked her life. Every morning she manages to dress herself and venture out into the world. Food has no taste, all of life is absent of true color, and all sound is garbled and enters her ear as a monotone drone.

Four months later her mother drops by the house on the weekend of her birthday. She really doesn't want to talk to anyone, and she certainly doesn't want to celebrate anything in life. But this is her mother, the one person she can't run away from. She enters the house and says, "Hello____ (insert *her mother's* favorite nickname here), how are you doing baby?" She manages to squeeze out the words, "I am doing fine, Mama." Her mother comes over and wraps her arms around her and immediately she's five years old again.

It has been years since her mother had hugged her like this, and immediately she begins sobbing uncontrollably. The more her daughter sobs, the tighter she hugs. In spite of her advanced age, she summoned the strength to grasp her daughter's entire body and provide a sense of security she hadn't felt in forty years. Finally her daughter begins to regain her composure and starts to mutter an apology for balling her eyes out. She releases her mother-bear grip and hands her daughter a tissue to wipe her face.

They both sit down, and her mother begins to speak: "Sweetheart, before you were conceived, I wanted you. Before you were born, I loved you. Before you were here an hour, I would have died for you. I have loved you with all my heart since the day you were conceived. Every hurt that you have endured in life has been my hurt." Her daughter's eyes well up with tears that flow like an earth cleansing spring rain.

Her mother caresses her hand and continues: "Every triumphant joy that you have experienced has been my joy. When you left home, I knew you'd encounter more joys and more hurts; although you haven't been able to share them all with me, I have

A Mother's Love

felt every one of them. I want you to know that there is nothing you can do to close the door of my heart to you. I love you, and I will always be here for you.

"When my grandson was born, my heart doubled in size to make room for him. I could not love him any more if he was my own son. My heart is hurting twice; once for the place he has in my heart and once for the place in my heart that I have for you. Your father and I raised you and your brother and sister to know God and to love him and love his word. We taught you all what God's Word has to say about the decision your son has made for his life. Neither his decision nor his partner's decision can change what God's Word has declared. God's wrath will be visited upon the unrighteous:

For this reason God gave them up to vile passions. For even their women exchanged the natural use for what is against nature. Likewise also the men, leaving the natural use of the woman, burned in their lust for one another, men with men committing what is shameful, and receiving in themselves the penalty of their error which was due (Rom. 1:26–27 [NKJV]).

You shall not lie with a male as with a woman. It is an abomination (Lev. 18:22 [NKJV]).

Do not defile yourselves with any of these things; for by all these the nations are defiled, which I am casting out before you. For the land is defiled; therefore I visit the punishment of its iniquity upon it, and the land vomits out its inhabitants. You shall therefore keep my statutes and my judgments, and shall not commit any of these abominations, either any of your own nation or any stranger who dwells among you (for all these abominations the men of the land have done, who were before you, and thus the land is defiled), lest the land vomit you out also when you defile it, as it vomited out the nations that were before you. For whoever commits any of these abominations, the persons who commit them shall be cut off from among their people (Lev. 18:24–29 [NKJV]).

If a man lies with a male as he lies with a woman, both of them have committed an abomination. They shall surely be put to death. Their blood shall be upon them (Lev. 20:13 [NKJV]).

Her daughter begins to sob as she is speaking. She pauses, remaining where she is seated, and then she continues: "Sweetheart, I know you're hurting. I imagine your stomach feels like someone has a meat grinder that's grinding up your intestines. But baby, you have a hard decision to make. Who are you going to stand with now; are you going to stand with God, or are you going to stand with your son? Growing up you all had to make some hard choices about dating, drinking, and premarital sex. But none of that can compare with this.

"When you all were young and felt shortchanged by life, do you remember what your father used to tell you? He would say, 'Life isn't fair, but God is merciful.' Sweetheart, please don't dwell on how unfair this situation is; that road only leads to a dead end: *despair*.

"Your remaining obedient to the Word of God is the only thing that can sustain you through this journey and give you any hope of restoring a Godly relationship with your son. You can go to him and embrace him and embrace his lifestyle; it will temporarily ease your pain, but you won't ever find any real happiness there. I have watched you and your husband raise that boy. You all have given him everything a young man needs to make his way in this world. He knows the Word of God...I remember the day he was baptized, and now he has made his choice to live outside of it. You have nothing in this world to feel guilty about—that's his choice, not yours. God's Word says if he, or any Christian refuses to repent, he must be cut off, and in order for you to remain obedient to God, you have no other choice.

"I wrote to you in my epistle not to keep company with sexually immoral people. Yet I certainly did not mean with the sexually immoral people of

*this world, or with the covetous, or idolaters, since then you would need to go out of the world. But now I have written to you **not to keep company with anyone named a brother**, who is sexually immoral, or covetous, or an idolater, or a reviler, or a drunkard, or an extortioner—not even to eat with such a person.*

*"For what have I to do with judging those also who are outside? Do you not judge those who are inside? But those who are outside, God judges. Therefore **put away from yourselves the evil person*** (1 Cor. 5:9–13 [NKJV]).

Her daughter begins to weep; her mother pauses, and then continues, "Honey, I know it sounds harsh. This is the last thing in the world that any mother wants to say to her daughter at a time like this. I suspect that it feels like you've been stabbed, and as you lie suffering in pain, I am twisting the knife. But I am your mother, and I am only telling you what God has mandated must be done. No mother that God has blessed with a child has the right to place their love for the child above their love and obedience to him, especially when that child has turned his back on God and has willfully chosen to live a sinful life."

Her mother gently caresses her hand and continues, "Honey, prayer is the most powerful option we have now. We will never stop loving him, and if he asks questions, because we are Christians, we must tell him what the Bible says and tell him we love him, but we also love God, and we trust and believe his holy Word to be true and right.

"Society is leading us to think that ways once viewed as wrong are now right. Well, what is popular is not always right, and what is right is certainly seldom popular. We must never stop loving him and never stop praying for him and for all those who are trapped in this sinful life. We must clearly communicate to him that although he will always have our love, he cannot have the full fellowship of our relationship until he repents of his sin.

"And have no fellowship with the unfruitful works of darkness, but rather expose them. For it is shameful even to speak of those things which are done by them in secret (Eph. 5:11–12 [NKJV]).

"Sweetheart, we cannot have *joint participation* in his sinful life. As harsh and unloving as this may sound to our human ears, God has assured us that this is the only true demonstration of our love for God and our love for him. If you could put both of our hearts together, there would not be enough love to gain repentance for him. If homosexuality is sinful, and indeed it is, there is only one heart that can gain repentance for him: *His.* Please don't use all the love in your heart trying to embrace him and his new life; keep enough love for God to enable you to be obedient and retain your own salvation.

*"If **You** love me, keep my commandments* (John 14:15 [NKJV]).

*"For **godly sorrow produces repentance** leading to salvation, not to be regretted; but the sorrow of the world produces death* (2 Cor. 7:10 [NKJV]).

*"I tell you, **no;** but **unless you repent** you will all likewise perish* (Luke 13:3 [NKJV]).

"The best thing for you to do now is speak up." Her daughter replied, "Mama, I can't talk right now." Her mother said, "Baby I don't mean speak to me …you need to speak to the world. Find a platform to speak to the next mother whose son ventures off into the darkness of homosexuality. Let her know that if she embraces him and his sin, she may very well lose him forever. Let the mothers of the world know, their only hope for a loving and fruitful relationship in this life is a mutual obedience to God by living in obedience to his word of truth. This is truly the greatest demonstration of a mother's love."

Speak truth freely, while it's still free.

STUDY GUIDE

Chapter 4: A Mother's Love

If you are a father, describe how you express your love for your child(ren).

If you are a father, have you ever felt that you had to compete against a mother's love?

If you are a mother, what are your impressions of bath time with your baby?

As a mother or father, what was your worst case of separation anxiety from your child?

During their son's formative years, should the mother or father have known something was different about their son? If they had, what could they have done about it?

After a year or so in college, should the mother or father have known something was different about their son? If they had known, what could they have done about it?

What do you think it must have felt like for the mother or father when he or she learned that his or her son was living a homosexual life?

What do you think the months of mental and emotional paralysis by the mother was like.

What are the similarities between what the grandmother said to her daughter and what the mother had previously said to her son?

Would you change anything about what the grandmother said to the mother?

Are the parents free to embrace, support, or continue in full relational fellowship with their son as he lives a homosexual life? Defend your position with scripture.

What does her mother believe is the most powerful option they have now? Is she right? Why or why not?

Can she and her mother love and pray her son out of sin? If not, how can he get out?

What was her mother's challenge to her? Is there any scripture that provides encouragement for Christians in a similar position as the mother to do likewise? If so, give an example.

What did her mother believe the danger was in embracing him in his sin? Is she right? Why or why not?

Personal take away:

_____

_____

_____

Chapter 5
OUTING CHRISTIANS

From the beginning Christianity and its followers were shunned and rejected by most people. Beginning as a sect among Jews, and according to the New Testament account, Pharisees, including Paul of Tarsus prior to his conversion, persecuted the early church. The first Christians preached a messiah who did not conform to the expectations of the time. However, feeling that He was prophesized in Isaiah's Suffering Servant and in all of Jewish scripture, Christians had been hopeful that their fellow citizens would accept their vision of a New Israel. Despite many individual conversions, they mostly found fierce opposition.

Dissension began almost immediately with the teachings of Stephen at Jerusalem and never ceased entirely before the city was destroyed. A short time after the crucifixion of Jesus, Stephen was stoned for his alleged transgressions with Saul (who later converted and was renamed Paul) looking on. The New Testament states that Paul was himself imprisoned on several occasions by Roman authorities, stoned by Pharisees and left for dead on one occasion, and was eventually taken as a prisoner to Rome. Peter and other early Christians were also imprisoned, beaten, and harassed.

The Jewish persecutions were trivial when compared with the brutal and widespread persecution by the Romans. Of the eleven remaining apostles (Judas Iscariot having killed himself), only one—John the son of Zebedee and the younger brother of the Apostle James—died of natural causes in exile. The other ten were reportedly martyred by various means including beheading, by sword and spear, and in the case of Peter, crucifixion upside down following the execution of his wife. The Romans were involved in some of these persecutions.

Persecution of the early church occurred sporadically almost from the beginning, but it was first sanctioned by the government under Nero. In 64 AD, a great fire ravaged Rome. Nero took the opportunity provided by the destruction to rebuild the city in the Greek style and began building a large palace for himself. People speculated that Nero had set the fire himself in order to indulge his aesthetic tastes in the reconstruction, so according to Tacitus's *Annals* and Suetonius's *Nero*, the eccentric emperor blamed the Christians for the fire in an effort to divert attention from him. Nero was quite insane and is reported to have tortured Christians with great cruelties for his own enjoyment.

According to the Roman historian Tacitus, besides being put to death they [the Christians] were made to serve as objects of amusement; they were clad in the hides of beast and torn to death by dogs; others were crucified, others set on fire to serve to illuminate the night when daylight failed. Nero had thrown open his grounds for the display, and was putting on a show in the circus, where he mingled with the people in the dress of a charioteer or drove about in his chariot. All this gave rise to a feeling of pity, even toward men whose guilt merited the most exemplary punishment; for it was felt that they were being destroyed not for the public good but to satisfy the cruelty of an individual.

Despite these extreme cruelties, Nero's persecution was local and short-lived. However, it was the first official persecution and marked the first time the government distinguished Christians

Outing Christians

from Jews. Tertullian referred to persecution of Christians as *institutum Neronianum*, an institution of Nero. After Nero, it became a capital crime to be a Christian, although pardon was always available if one publicly condemned Christ and sacrificed to the gods.

The Roman Empire was generally quite tolerant in its treatment of other religions. The imperial policy was generally one of incorporation—the local gods of a newly conquered area were simply added to the Roman pantheon and often given Roman names. Even the Jews, with their one god, were generally tolerated. So why the persecution of Christians?

In order to understand the Roman distrust of Christianity, one must understand the Roman view of religion. For the Romans, religion was first and foremost a social activity that promoted unity and loyalty to the state—a religious attitude the Romans called *pietas*, or piety. Cicero wrote that if piety in the Roman sense were to disappear, social unity and justice would perish along with it.

The early Roman writers viewed Christianity not as another kind of *pietas*, or piety, but as a *superstitio*, "superstition." Pliny, a Roman governor writing circa 110 AD, called Christianity a "superstition taken to extravagant lengths." Similarly, the Roman historian Tacitus called it "a deadly superstition," and the historian Suetonius called Christians "a class of persons given to a new and mischievous superstition." In this context, the word "superstition" has a slightly different connotation than it has today: for the Romans, it designated something foreign and different, in a negative sense. Religious beliefs were valid only in so far as they could be shown to be old and in line with ancient customs; new and innovative teachings were regarded with distrust.

The Roman distaste for Christianity, then, arose in large part from their sense *that it was bad for society*. In the third century, the

Neoplatonist philosopher Porphyry wrote, "How can people not be in every way impious and atheistic who have apostatized from the customs of our ancestors through which every nation and city is sustained? What else are they than fighters against God?" (Religionfacts.com - Persecution in the Early Church)

Persecution lasted until Constantine I legalized Christianity in 313. It was not until Theodosius I in the later fourth century that Christianity would become the official religion of the Roman Empire. Between these two events, Julian II temporarily restored the traditional Roman religion and established broad religious tolerance, renewing Pagan and Christian hostilities.

In the twentieth century, Christians were persecuted by various groups and by atheistic states such as Russia and North Korea. The Christian missionary organization Open Doors (UK) estimates 100 million Christians face persecution, particularly in Muslim-dominated countries such as Pakistan and Saudi Arabia. A survey reported in 2010 that at least 75 percent of religious persecution reported from 2008–2010 around the world was directed at people of the Christian faith.

Since its inception the United States of America has occupied a unique position in the world as it relates to religious persecution. Our founding fathers were very familiar with religious persecution and wrote religious freedom into the constitution: *The First Amendment to the United States Constitution prohibits the making of any law respecting an establishment of religion, impeding the free exercise of religion…*

Once more, in 2014, the United States is grappling with religious liberty, as Christians try to express their religious beliefs in response to the homosexual agenda. Their advocates are pressing for open expression and acceptance of their lifestyle including all the rights and privileges of marriage. In today's jaded culture there is a deeply engrained cynicism toward religious followers who speak out against any particular sin. In response, Christians, *for the most part,* have retreated from the public square to the safe confines of their houses of worship. One might wonder if today's Christians actually know the history of persecution inflicted upon members of their faith.

Many Christians are afraid to speak up because they don't consider themselves to be perfect. They have forgotten their credibility doesn't lie with the world; it resides with God. In order to possess the credibility to stand against unrighteousness, you have to live a life that is consistent with the beliefs you espouse. Given that you're human, you will fall, however, through godly sorrow (2 Cor. 7:9); God allows everyone to repent and thereby be restored to full fellowship with him or to be made perfect or complete in his eyes.

God is not asking us to save the world; he has done that already by sending his son to die on the cross. He only asks that we use our life to bear fruits of righteousness:

Every tree that does not bear good fruit is cut down and thrown into the fire. Therefore by their fruits you will know them. Not everyone who says to me, "Lord, Lord," shall enter the kingdom of heaven, **but he who does the will of my Father in heaven***. Many will say to me in that day, "Lord, Lord, have we not prophesied in Your name, cast out demons in Your name, and done many wonders in Your name?" And then I will declare to them, "I never knew you; depart from me, you who practice lawlessness"* (Matt. 7:19–23 [NKJV])!

You are the salt of the earth; but if the salt loses its flavor, how shall it be seasoned? It is then good for nothing but to be thrown out and trampled underfoot by men. **You are the light of the world***. A city that is set on a hill cannot be hidden. Nor do they light a lamp and put it under a basket, but on a lampstand, and it gives light to all who are in the house. Let your light so shine before men, that they may see your good works and glorify your Father in heaven* (Matt. 5:13–16 [NKJV]).

Advocates for the homosexual movement have made strategic use of media to sway public opinion and public sentiment in their favor. Several laws have been enacted to give legitimacy to their lifestyle and insulate them against adverse speech and actions. Over the past generation they have made alliances in the entertainment industry, business community, the world of politics, and that of religion. These alliances were then leveraged to garner political votes and judicial decisions to add the rule of law as fortification for their desire to live freely and openly homosexual in America.

In some respects Christians and homosexuals have switched places. Fifty years ago homosexuals were in the closet, and Christians were living free and open. Today homosexuals are living free and open, and Christians, at a minimum, have at least one foot in the closet. Today Christians are not free to express their religious view that homosexuality is sin in many workplaces without fear of reprisal. A Christian who dares to speak against homosexuality at work stands a very real chance of being disciplined, possibly to the extent of being fired. Could this be the fruit of a generation of silence?

Elisabeth Noelle-Neumann, a German political scientist, developed a political science and mass communication theory known as the **spiral of silence**. This theory describes the process by which, over time, one opinion becomes dominant as those who perceive their opinion to be in the minority don't speak up because society threatens individuals with fear of rebuke and isolation.

Three conditions are necessary for the spiral of silence to occur:

- The issue must have a moral component to it.
- There is a time factor or dynamic aspect of public opinion.
- There is constant and ongoing mass media coverage.

The Spiral Model

1. As social beings, most people are afraid of becoming isolated from their environment. They would like to be popular and respected.

2. In order to avoid becoming isolated and in order not to lose popularity and esteem, people constantly observe their environment very closely. They try to find out which opinions and modes of behavior are prevalent, and which opinions and modes of behavior are becoming more popular. They behave and express themselves accordingly in public.

3. We can distinguish between fields where the opinions and attitudes involved are static and fields where those opinions and attitudes are subject to changes. Where opinions are relatively definite and static—for example, "customs"—one has to express or act according to this opinion in public or run the risk of becoming isolated. In contrast, where opinions are in flux, or disputed, the individual will try to find out which opinion he or she can express without becoming isolated.

4. Individuals who, when observing their environments, notice that their own personal opinions are spreading and are being taken over by others, will voice this opinion self-confidently in public. On the other hand, individuals who notice that their own opinions are losing ground will be inclined to adopt a more reserved attitude when expressing their opinions in public.

5. It follows from this that, as the representatives of the first opinion talk quite a lot, while the representatives of the second opinion remain silent, there is a definite influence on the environment: an opinion that is being

reinforced in this way appears stronger than it really is, while an opinion suppressed as described will seem to be weaker than it is in reality.

6. The result is a spiral process that prompts other individuals to perceive the changes in opinion and follow suit, until one opinion has become established as the prevailing attitude, while the other opinion will be pushed back and rejected by everybody with the exception of the hard core people who nevertheless stick to their opinions.

The spiral of silence theory holds that the silence is broken by a vocal minority (the complement of the silent majority). It further states that this minority is a necessary factor of change, while the silent (compliant) majority is a necessary factor of stability. The vocal minority remains at the top of the spiral in defiance of threats of rebuke or isolation. The theory calls these vocal minorities the *hardcore nonconformists*. They are "people who have already been rejected for their beliefs and have nothing to lose by speaking out." Isn't this the position of Christians? The Bible commands Christians to fear God and not the world (Matt. 10:28); therefore, they have absolutely nothing to lose by breaking the spiral of silence and speaking truth freely.

On the issue of homosexuality in general and homosexual marriage in particular, Christians are called to be hardcore nonconformist. *We must remain steadfast and unmovable in our efforts to show love and respect to all humanity.* However, our love for humanity must never cause us to lessen our defiance of anyone who willfully disobeys God's commands and refuses to repent and turn from their sin. In fact, nothing could be more unloving than for a Christian to choose silence over lovingly sharing God's truths in an effort to lead one out of the darkness of sin and into God's marvelous light.

Outing Christians

Although the following scriptures are written to the evangelist Timothy, they are no less applicable to modern-day Christians, who are God's royal priesthood:

I charge thee therefore before God, and the Lord Jesus Christ, who shall judge the quick and the dead at his appearing and his kingdom; Preach the word; be instant in season, out of season; reprove, rebuke, exhort with all long suffering and doctrine. For the time will come when they will not endure sound doctrine; but after their own lusts shall they heap to themselves teachers, having itching ears; And they shall turn away their ears from the truth, and shall be turned unto fables (2 Tim. 4:1–4 [(KJV]).

In the first century the apostles and disciples were constantly subjected to punishments intended to silence them:

And they agreed with him, and when they had called for the apostles and beaten them, they **commanded that they should not speak in the name of Jesus***, and let them go. So they departed from the presence of the council, rejoicing that they were counted worthy to suffer shame for His name. And daily in the temple, and in every house, they did not cease teaching and preaching Jesus as the Christ* (Acts 5:40–42 [NKJV]).

The takeaway from the apostle's example in scripture is that: *We ought to obey God rather than men (Acts 5:29).* This we must do in all aspects of our lives. Of course, you're not compelled at work to be the spiritual cop for your department. You're at work first and foremost to do a job. But, anyone with the inclination to ask your viewpoint on any spiritual subject matter must be told *what thus saith the Lord.* You can't sugar coat it or mushy mouth it; they asked, and you must tell it, *book, chapter, and verse.*

And who is he who will harm you if you become followers of what is good? But even if you should suffer for righteousness's sake, you are blessed. And do not be afraid of their threats, nor be troubled. But sanctify the Lord God in your hearts, and **always be ready to give a defense** *to everyone* *who asks you a reason for the hope that is in you, with meekness and fear; having a good conscience, that when they defame you as evildoers, those who revile your good conduct in Christ may be ashamed.* **For it is better, if it is the will of God, to suffer for doing good than for doing evil** (1 Pet. 3:13–17 [NKJV]).

From the beginning of Christianity, Christians have suffered persecution, and the persecution continues in many parts of the world to this day. In the United States, Christians are in the early stages of an eventual all-out assault by those advocating for the homosexual agenda. Their goal is unfettered access to all rights and privileges in marriage, including free and unrestrained expression of the homosexual lifestyle in all of society.

As it is with all movements, homosexlual advocates on the fringe are levying blatantly false assertions and character assassinations against the Christian community. Rarely do these voices resonate outside of the blogosphere. But, over the past twenty years or so, advocates have carefully crafted a mainstream campaign that used two buzz words to reframe the public debate: *tolerance and political correctness*. With the soil sufficiently tilled, they coopted the term *homophobia* coined by George Weinberg, a psychologist, in the 1960s.

So today if a Christian dares to utter a word against homosexuality outside the friendly confines of their house of worship, they are labeled with a false psychological malady (homophobia). Homosexual advocates are simply engaging in a grade school bullying tactic: *name calling*. And as it is on the elementary playground, if you don't defend yourself against name calling, things will get physical at some point. In school, teachers are the intermediaries who come to your defense. As Christians if you take a stand, God will defend you.

Fear not, for I am with you; be not dismayed, for I am your God. I will strengthen you, Yes, I will help you, I will uphold you with my righteous right hand. (Isa. 41:10 [NKJV]).

Although you're not called to be a prophet like Isaiah, the gospel does demand that you take a stand against all unrighteousness. Homosexuality is sinful, it is time to speak up; the Bible and the US constitution have got your back.

Speak truth freely, while it's still free.

STUDY GUIDE

Chapter 5: Outing Christians

Describe the persecution that Christians were subjected to during the time of Saul of Tarsus.

Describe the persecution that Christians were subjected to under Nero.

After Nero Christianity became a capital crime, although a pardon could be gained by doing what?

The Roman Empire was generally tolerant in its treatment of other religions. Why did it respond harshly to Christianity?

The Romans believed Christianity was bad for society. Is Christianity bad for our postmodern twenty-first century American society? Why or why not?

Are there inherent conflicts between religious freedom and freedom to live as one chooses? If so, how do we as a nation navigate through these conflicts?

Are Christians compelled to take an active stand against sinful influences in society? Defend your position with scripture.

Describe some of the tactics used by advocates of the homosexual agenda to fortify their position.

What is the definition of the spiral of silence?

What are the three conditions necessary for the spiral of silence to occur?

Discuss items four, five, and six of the spiral of silence model.

As it relates to the public debate on homosexual marriage, should Christians be in the vocal minority or the compliant majority? Why?

How would you convince someone that it is better to risk the reprisals from speaking publicly against homosexuality rather than remaining silent (I Pet. 3:13–17)?

Is there any potential future danger to Christians in not responding to the homosexual advocates' campaign of name calling?

Personal take away:

_____

_____

_____

Chapter 6

HOMOSEXUALITY: HUMAN RIGHTS AND HUMAN WRONGS

Some say that sexual orientation and gender identity are sensitive issues. I understand. Like many of my generation, I did not grow up talking about these issues. But I learned to speak out because lives are at stake, and because it is our duty under the United Nations Charter and the Universal Declaration of Human Rights to protect the rights of everyone, everywhere.

UN Secretary-General Ban Ki-moon to the Human Rights Council, 7 March 2012

The United Nations Human Rights Council defines human rights as: "rights inherent to all human beings, whatever our nationality, place of residence, sex, national or ethnic origin, color, religion, language, or any other status." Universal human rights are often expressed and guaranteed by law, in the forms of treaties, customary international law, general principles and other sources of international law. International human rights law lays down obligations of governments to act in certain ways or to refrain from certain acts, in order to promote and protect human rights and fundamental freedoms of individuals or groups.

The principle of universality of human rights is the cornerstone of international human rights law. This principle, as first emphasized in the Universal Declaration on Human Rights in 1948, has been reiterated in numerous international human rights conventions, declarations, and resolutions. The 1993 Vienna World Conference on Human Rights, for example, noted that it is the duty of States to promote and protect all human rights and fundamental freedoms, regardless of their political, economic and cultural systems.

Currently, deeply embedded cultural attitudes, often combined with a lack of adequate legal protection against discrimination on grounds of sexual orientation and gender identity, expose LGBT people of all ages and in all regions of the world to egregious violations of their human rights. They are discriminated against in the labor market, in schools and in hospitals, mistreated and disowned by their own families. They are singled out for physical attack—beaten, sexually assaulted, tortured and killed. And in some seventy-six countries, discriminatory laws criminalize private, consensual same-sex relationships—exposing individuals to the risk of arrest, prosecution, imprisonment—even, in at least five countries, the death penalty.

Concerns about these and related human rights violations have been expressed repeatedly by United Nations human rights mechanisms since the early 1990s. These mechanisms include the treaty bodies established to monitor states' compliance with international human rights treaties, as well as the special rapporteurs and other independent experts appointed by the Human Rights Council to investigate and report on pressing human rights challenges.

In December 2010, Ban Ki-moon the secretary-general delivered a landmark speech on LGBT equality in New York calling for the worldwide decriminalization of homosexuality and for other measures to tackle violence and discrimination against LGBT people. "As men and women of conscience, we reject discrimination in general, and in particular discrimination based on sexual orientation and gender identity. *Where there is tension between cultural attitudes and universal human rights, rights must carry the day,*" he said.

Protecting LGBT people from violence and discrimination does not require the creation of a new set of LGBT-specific rights, nor does it require the establishment of new international human rights standards. The legal obligations of states to safeguard the human rights of LGBT people are well established in international human rights law on the basis of the Universal Declaration of Human Rights and subsequently agreed international human rights treaties.

All people, irrespective of sex, sexual orientation or gender identity, are entitled to enjoy the protections provided for by international human rights law, including in respect of rights to life, security of person and privacy, the right to be free from torture, arbitrary arrest and detention, the right to be free from discrimination and the right to freedom of expression, association and peaceful assembly. There you have it, the case for protecting and defending homosexuals throughout the world on the grounds of their human rights.

*For this reason God gave them up to vile passions. For even their women exchanged the natural use for what is against nature. Likewise also the men, leaving the **natural use** of the woman, burned in their lust for one another, men with men committing what is shameful, and receiving in themselves the penalty of their error which was due* (Rom. 1:26–27 [NKJV]).

You shall not lie with a male as with a woman. It is an abomination (Lev. 18:22 [NKJV]).

Homosexuality: Human Rights And Human Wrongs

A > B and B > C
What do we know about the relationship between A and C?

A: Homosexuality is sin.
B: Abusing homosexuals is wrong.
C: Is homosexuality sin?

The logic constructs above come out of a time, just thirty or forty short years ago, when there was almost universal agreement on what the right answers were. However, for the past thirty years or so, the Christian community has allowed homosexual advocates to drive the public conversation. They have been allowed to redefine the word "natural" and expand the concept of "human rights." *We are living in an age when intelligent people are asserting the proposition that two men, who meet and fall in love, should have the human right to marry, and raise and nurture a family if they so choose.*

This writing is written to and intended for a Christian audience. The objective herein is to equip them as they defend the proposition that homosexuality is sin. *No human being has a **right** to disobey God's principles and natural design then assert that they also have the right to compel society to sanction their sinful lifestyle.* If a society has so chosen to establish laws based upon and that upholds God's moral standards are they not free to criminalize any behavior forbidden by God? Furthermore, religion aside, a democratic people are free to so order their lives in any manner deemed reasonable and proper by a majority of its citizens.

Therefore the question of whether homosexual marriage is constitutional or unconstitutional is irrelevant in a Godless context. As atheist Jean-Paul Sartre once affirmed, *Everything is indeed permitted if God does not exist.* Unfortunately, the dominance of secularism and the expansion of the separation principle between church and state have filled with fear and dread any person who dares to reference deity or "natural law"…at all.

My people are destroyed for lack of knowledge. Because you have rejected knowledge, I also will reject you from being priest for me; because you have forgotten the law of your God, I also will forget your children (Hosea 4:6 [NKJV]).

Although the prophet Hosea is speaking to the people about their lack of knowledge of God's law, the past generation in America has seemingly brought a decline in knowledge in general. Reading of any kind has all but been replaced by reality TV, video games, and the latest big-screen blockbuster movie.

When was the last time you heard of someone reading a natural science book or a *National Geographic* magazine article on nature? The following definitions are presented as a refresher: (*Random House Dictionary*)

Nature: the material world, especially as surrounding humankind and existing independently of human activities. *Idiom*: by nature, as a result of inborn or inherent qualities; innately: *She is by nature a kindhearted person.*

Natural: noun: any person or thing that is or is likely, or certain to be very suitable to and successful in an endeavor without much training or difficulty; adj: existing in or formed by nature (opposed to artificial): a natural bridge; following or resembling nature or life; lifelike: *She looked more natural without her makeup.*

Somewhere around middle school, you started to learn about the laws of the universe. Remember the popular story that Isaac Newton was sitting under an apple tree, an apple fell on his head, and he suddenly thought of the universal law of gravitation? As in all such legends, this is almost certainly not true in its details, but the story contains elements of what actually happened. Probably the more correct version of the story is that Newton, upon observing an apple fall from a tree, began to think along the following lines: the apple accelerates, since its velocity changes from zero as it is hanging on the tree and moves toward the ground.

Thus, by Newton's second law there must be a force that acts on the apple to cause this acceleration. Let's call this force "gravity" and the associated acceleration the "acceleration due to gravity." Then imagine the apple tree is twice as high. Again, we expect the apple to accelerate toward the ground, so this suggests that this force that we call gravity reaches to the top of the tallest apple tree.

Most kids (boys in particular) do not want to be subject to the law of gravity. They start by jumping off the couch, the stairs, porch railings, the garage, or a tree limb; somewhere along the way they encounter some pain, hopefully not a broken limb. A parent sits them down and explains that God created gravity for our benefit. Without gravity we would fly off into space and burn up. Generally, this conversation isn't enough to stop them from trying to defy gravity, so the parent has to monitor and guide them until they reach the age where they buy in for their own safety.

What if one little fellow never grew out of that stage? How would you respond to a seventeen-year-old who said, "I don't want to be subject to the law of gravity? I want to jump out of a ten-story building and suffer no more harm than if I jumped off the curb"? Not wanting to be limited by the laws of nature will prove problematic for this young man's life.

God's law of human nature at creation is that we are born male and female. He created humankind with the natural predisposition toward opposite sex attractions in which relationships are formed that result in procreation. Same-sex attraction philosophically violates this law, and if carried to its logical end, would eventually lead to the extinction of the human species.

The assertion often is made that homosexuals deserve equal rights just as other minority groups do, and should not be punished for, or forbidden from, expressing their homosexuality. The fight for the acceptance of homosexuality often is compared to "civil rights" movements of racial minorities. In America's failure to settle fully the civil rights issue (i.e., full and equal citizenship of racial minorities), homosexual advocates were provided with the perfect "coat tail" to ride to advance their agenda. *By the way, what happened to all the "gay only" bathroom and water fountain signs?* Nevertheless, using the camouflage of civil liberties, homosexual activists were able to divert attention away from the behavior and focus it on the "right" to engage in the behavior. Slick, huh?

The argument goes like this: "Just as a person cannot help being black, female, or Asian, I cannot help being homosexual. We were all born this way, and as such we should be treated equally." However, this argument fails to comprehend the true "civil rights" movements. The law already protects the civil rights of everyone—black, white, male, female, homosexual, or heterosexual. Homosexuals enjoy the same civil rights as everyone else. Their contention arises when specific laws deprive *all citizens* from engaging in certain behaviors (e.g., sodomy). We should keep in mind that these laws are the same for all members of society. Because of certain deprivations, homosexuals feel as though "equal" rights have been taken away (e.g., marriage, tax breaks).

For African Americans and everyone else, skin color and other genetic traits can be traced through inheritance patterns and simple Mendelian genetics. Homosexuals are *identified* not by a trait or a gene, but rather by their actions. Without the actions, they would be indistinguishable from all other people. It is only when they alter their behavior that they become a group that is recognized as being different. If we were to assume momentarily that homosexuality was genetic, the most one could conclude is that those individuals were not morally responsible for *being* homosexual.

However, that does not mean that they are not morally responsible for homosexual actions! Merely having the gene does not force one to carry out the behavior. For instance, many African Americans inherit a genetic predisposition toward high blood pressure and diabetes. Yet, if a person develops the self-discipline to live a healthy lifestyle (diet and exercise), they often avoid all together or, at a minimum, delay the effects of these maladies until far later in life.

For millions of African Americans, the choice to live their life free and open to all the foods they want to eat comes with a lifetime of pain and suffering for themselves and their families. Those who exhibit the self-control to eat a balanced diet free of excesses are rewarded with a substantially higher quality of life than those who allow their passion for food to rule over them.

The key determinant in a person's life is not his or her genetic predispositions; rather it is whether or not a person chooses to live in a way that exacerbates the negative effects of those predispositions. The real issue here is homosexual actions that God deems sinful, and in many instances, societies the world over consider illegal. Homosexuals and heterosexuals are both equally prohibited by God from engaging in fornication. Homosexuals are no different than every man who chooses not to take a wife and every woman who chooses not to take a husband; they all have to develop the self-discipline and self-control necessary to live a life of abstinence.

Homosexuality goes against human nature in at least two fundamental ways. First, on a basic physical, anatomical level, homosexuality disregards the natural use of the sexual organs of men and women. Humans were designed to be sexually compatible in order to reproduce and bear offspring (Gen. 1:28). If homosexuality were a natural genetic occurrence, the genes responsible for it would quickly disappear due to the inability of same-sex couples to reproduce.

Second, God designed men and women to be capable of a relationship in marriage unlike any other human relationship. When a man and a woman are joined together, they become "one flesh," a biblical phrase that describes the epitome of intimacy and compatibility (Gen. 2:23).

God specifically designed Eve, and all future women, to be perfect helpers suitable for Adam and all subsequent men. And while it is true that sinful humans often fail to achieve the intimacy and oneness designed by God, it is not because of faulty design but because of people's sinful decisions. God designed men and women to be naturally compatible both physically and emotionally.

In recent years it has become fashionable for advocates to suggest that homosexuality is legitimized by the fact that some animals act in this manner. If human behavior can be justified based on the supposition that similar behavior is found in the animal kingdom, then why not abolish all laws, allow stronger humans to kill the weaker ones, allow mothers to eat their babies, allow men to murder sexual rivals, allow women to murder and cannibalize their lovers after intercourse, and simply chalk up such a deplorable situation to "*nature*"?

The logical consequences of such a philosophical justification are as obvious as they are ridiculous. God created humans, so he knows what is in accordance with human nature, and he has clearly stated that homosexuality is abominable, unnatural, sinful behavior (Rom. 1:26–27, Lev. 18:22).

The United Nations is to be applauded for its work. This organization has done much to advance the cause of human dignity and stop ruthless governments, dictators, and regimes from inflicting brutality on their people. While it remains true that there are those throughout the world who discriminate against and inflict physical harm upon individuals who choose to live the homosexual lifestyle, it also remains true that the God of creation is equally as grieved by the sinful lifestyle of homosexuality as he is by those who unlawfully mistreat them.

The United Nations is staffed and run by people of goodwill who are seeking to make the world a better place. Like millions of other people, they are unable to separate the advancement of true human rights issues from the advancement of the sinful cause of homosexuals. Homosexual advocates have been shrewd and beguiling in their strategies to coopt the efforts of others to advance their agenda.

If at this point you have concluded that the objective herein is to suggest we abolish the United Nations and allow homosexuals the world over to fend for themselves, you have completely missed the point. There are always unintended consequences of almost every action that we as humans take. There is an old saying that goes: "two wrongs don't make a right." It would be wrong for the United Nations to stop defending homosexuals from those who would persecute them. However, is it also wrong for the United Nations to *never* address the pain and suffering that millions the world over inflict upon themselves by living this sinful lifestyle?

What now? There is an old quote that says, "knowing is half the battle." No one can expect anyone to change or respond to what they don't know. But when one knows, the other half of the battle is finding the will to do something about it.

Therefore, to one who knows the right thing to do and does not do it, to him it is sin (James 4:17 [NASB]).

Speak truth freely, while it's still free.

STUDY GUIDE

Chapter 6: Homosexuality: Human Rights and Human Wrongs

What is the United Nations's definition of human rights? Do you have any disagreements with this definition?

Describe how homosexuals are mistreated in the world.

Do you agree or disagree with the following statement made by United Nations Secretary-General Ban Ki-moon: "Where there is tension between cultural attitudes and universal human rights, rights must carry the day." (Bear in mind, around the world religion plays a huge role in shaping cultural attitudes.)

How did this book describe the case for protecting and defending homosexuals throughout the world on the grounds of their human rights? Do you agree or disagree? Why or why not?

Describe how God's law of gravity works. What are the inherent dangers for us when we disobey?

Describe God's law of human nature at creation. What happens if humans disobey God's law?

If a society has chosen to establish laws based upon, and that uphold, God's moral codes, are they not free to criminalize any behavior outlawed by God? Why or why not?

What is the logical end-state for humanity if same-sex relationships were allowed to flourish?

Describe the rationale behind linking the homosexual movement with the African American civil rights movement. How successful has this strategy been? Should one be offended by this strategy?

Describe how this rationale is shown to be blatantly false.

Apart from their actions, what distinguishes homosexuals from everyone else?

Are human beings destined to live out all of the manifestations of their genetic predispositions? If not, what is required of them to live a life of obedience to God?

What are the two fundamental ways that homosexuality goes against human nature?

Discuss the logical implications surrounding the stance that homosexuality is legitimized by the fact that some animals act in this manner.

Describe how a society that is seeking to live by Godly principles might go about protecting homosexuals from abuse without sanctioning their lifestyle.

www.SpeakTruthFreely.com   *While it's still free!*

Personal take away:

_____

_____

_____

Chapter 7
GRANDPARENTS

Throughout history grandparents have played an important role in stablizing society and faciliting the transference of morals and values. Historically, as well as today, in many countries they are included in the definition of the basic family unit. In an extended family, parents and their children's families may often live under one roof. For many cultures around the world, such as some in Asia, Africa, Eastern Europe and the Pacific Islands, extended families are the basic family unit.

Australian aborigines are another group for whom the concept of family extends well beyond the nuclear model (one set of adult parents and their children; *Merriam-Webster Unabridged*). Aboriginal immediate families include aunts, uncles, and a number of other relatives who would be considered "distant relations" in the context of the nuclear family. Their family structure incorporates a shared responsibility for all tasks. Where families consist of multiple generations living together, the family is usually headed by the oldest man. More often than not, it consists of grandparents, their sons, and their sons' families.

In the joint family setup, the patriarch of the family (often the oldest male member) lays down the rules and arbitrates disputes. Senior female members of the household babysit infants when their mother is working. They are also responsible for teaching the younger children how to speak, manners, and etiquette. Grandparents often take the leading roles due to the fact that they have the most experience with parenting and maintaining a household.

Recent trends in the United States have seen an increase in multigenerational households. Results of a study by Pew Research Center in 2010 revealed that approximately 50 million (nearly one in six) Americans, including rising numbers of seniors, live in households with at least two adult generations and often three. It has become an ongoing trend for elderly generations to move in and live with their children, as they can give them support and help with everyday living. The main reasons cited for this shift are increase in unemployment, slumped housing prices, and the arrival of new family members immigranting from another country. But, in the majority of cases the grandparents are the householders who bring their adult children and grandchildren into their home.

Historically American grandparents had just one role: spoil their grandchildren. The *rottener* the better! The results of a recent AARP survey of grandparents highlighted the roles they play in the lives of their grandchildren, and 90 percent say that role is an important one. Surveyed grandparents were asked about their roles and the importance of their relationships with their grandchildren. Spoiling the grandkids is by far at the top (36 percent)—this view has stayed consistent over the years. It's the only role that grandparents seem to think is more theirs than that of the parents or at least shared between grandparents and parents.

Coming in second is teaching their grandchildren about family history (28 percent), although 66 percent see sharing family history as a dual role between parents and grandparents. Another role grandparents see for themselves is giving special treats and gifts (28 percent).

American grandparents also still spend significant dollars on their grandchildren: 40 percent report spending more than $500 on their grandchildren over the last 12 months. The most common reason grandparents say they spend money on grandchildren is birthdays and holidays (95 percent.) No big surprise there. But a significant number of grandparents also provide necessities and critical support for their grandchildren, which create a safety net for grandchildren when parents can't quite take care of the basics, including:

- 53 percent contribute to education costs
- 37 percent help with everyday living expenses
- 23 percent pay medical or dental bills

Despite the economy most grandparents agree they would make sacrifices rather than let their financial situation adversely affect their grandchildren.

By any name they are no less precious; however, not everyone likes the terms "grandma" and "grandpa." Although those were the most popular grandparent nicknames in a recent survey, respondents also cited nicknames like "Nana," "Papa," "Granny," "Granddad," "Mimi," "Poppy," "Big Mama," and "Big Daddy."

Regardless of what you called them, grandparents hold a special place in the hearts of almost everyone for whom they played a role in their early lives. These are people who said things like, "Sure you can have another piece of candy, it'll be our little secret," "This is the last time I'm going to pick up your toys," "OK, just one more story and you have to go to sleep," or "If you stop crying I'll buy you a _____." How can you not completely love someone who resorts to bribery as a means to make you happy?

Going to their house was better than going to an amusement park. Nana and Papa were your personal entertainment guides. Both of them had their special activities they wanted to do with you. Whether it was the classics of baking cookies with Nana or going fishing with Papa, their house was your personal Disneyland. Their house had a certain smell that many of us will take to our graves. Regardless of how big or small, their house was overflowing with hugs, kisses, and nothing but l-o-v-e for y-o-u.

A grandparent can be the caring adult who loves unconditionally and provides that listening ear that all kids need, which helps shape who they become as adults. When you are a kid and you're trying to figure out who you are and who you might become, you need to have *a menu of the choices.* You need someone to do something or say something that resonates to the core of your being. It is this spark that ignites a fire inside you that burns brightly, and if you live a thousand lifetimes, you could not exhaust the flame.

Grandparents are quite often the first people to notice, appreciate, and encourage your core gifts and talents. They are charter members of your first fan club. When you're three years old, and granddad tosses you a plastic ball that you hit two out of three times, he loses his mind and acts as though you drove in the winning run in the World Series. Granny is overcome with emotion after you give her a personal ballerina dance recital. These are the people who encourage you to follow your heart, not to listen to the naysayers, and to chart your own course in this world. They are convinced, and will do everything within their power to convince you, that you have greatness within you.

The Bible is clear on the importance of family, and a grandma or grandpa can use their maturity and wisdom to help influence grandchildren for Christ. As children grow older, they remember the way some of their role models lived and they try to model their own lives after them. A Christian grandparent is a great role model for the younger generation. The Bible has two role model examples in which a grandchild was impacted by the grandparent's actions:

In the twentieth year of Jeroboam king of Israel, Asa became king over Judah. And he reigned forty-one years in Jerusalem. His grandmother's name was Maachah the granddaughter of Abishalom. Asa did what was right in the eyes of the Lord, as did his father David. And he banished the perverted persons from the land, and removed all the idols that his fathers had made. Also he removed Maachah his grandmother from being queen mother because she had made an obscene image of Asherah. And Asa cut down her obscene image and burned it by the Brook Kidron. But the high places were not removed. Nevertheless Asa's heart was loyal to the Lord all his days (1 Kings 15:9–14 [NKJV]).

The last thing in the world a grandparent should ever be to his or her grandchild is an evil influence. Fortunately Asa's heart was loyal to God, so much so that his grandmother's influence could not turn him from being loyal all his days.

*Paul, an apostle of Jesus Christ by the will of God, according to the promise of life which is in Christ Jesus, To Timothy, a beloved son: Grace, mercy, and peace from God the Father and Christ Jesus our Lord. I thank God, whom I serve with a pure conscience, as my forefathers did, as without ceasing I remember you in my prayers night and day, greatly desiring to see you, being mindful of your tears, that I may be filled with joy, when I call to remembrance the genuine faith that is in you, which dwelt first in your **grandmother Lois** and your mother Eunice, and I am persuaded is in you also. Therefore I remind you to stir up the gift of God, which is in you through the laying on of my hands. For God has not given us a spirit of fear, but of power and of love and of a sound mind* (2 Tim. 1:1–7 [NKJV]).

Timothy's grandmother Lois is the kind of granny every young lady and young man needs. The young people of today need someone who first is uncompromising when it comes to holding them accountable to God's Word and second who they know loves them without question. Young people are vulnerable to all types of sinful lifestyles, of which homosexuality is certainly one. Although their hearts are breaking when a grandchild chooses to live in sin, faithful grandparents must stand with God. They do so by letting their grandchild know that they must repent and embrace a life of obedience to God.

Christian grandparents are the world's last best line of defense against the homosexuality movement. You have witnessed the changes that have occurred over the last thirty years. You remember a time when the politically correct thing to do was to be ashamed of one's sin; and you certainly never dreamed there'd come a time when someone would engage in sin and proclaim that he or she has a human right to demand total acceptance by society.

Only be careful, and watch yourselves closely so that you do not forget the things your eyes have seen or let them fade from your heart as long as you live. **Teach them to your children and to their children after them** (Deut. 4:9 [NKJV]).

In Deuteronomy, chapter 4, Moses is preparing Israel to go into the land that God had promised to them. God, through Moses, tells the children of Israel that future generations will remain obedient to him if they teach them about the things God has done for Israel. In Deuteronomy 6:7 Moses adds emphasis by telling Israel to teach them diligently!

God was well aware of the critical role grandparents played in society. Moses spoke to grandparents, charging them to pass on God's statues and judgments to future generations. Grandparents are the only ones who can stand in today and see the future through eyes from the past. *One generation shall praise your works to another, And shall declare your mighty acts* (Ps. 145:4).

Grandparents have witnessed the righteous not forsaken (Ps. 37:25) and have seen calamity visited upon the wicked (Prov. 24:16). The wisdom grandparents have amassed through the years reassures them that *the fruits of sin for a season* are not to be compared with the rewards of a life lived in Christ or the eternal joy to be had thereafter.

In every age a grandparent's life and influence plays a vital role in determining the legacy that he or she leaves behind. This was true for the nation of Israel, and it remains especially true for our nation today. The United States is in desperate need of godly grandparents to declare God's mighty acts to their children and their children's children.

If your legacy is not what you want it to be, now is not the time to throw your hands up in despair. Regardless of how things stood with an erring grandchild when you started reading this book, if they are still on earth, you have a chance to make a positive impact for God. If you have been blessed with faithful children and grandchildren, consider the condition of our country and become an advocate for higher morals so that someone else's legacy may improve.

God blessed you to be born and raised in a god-fearing nation (although scholars still debate whether it was ever a Christian nation). But, there is no debate regarding the fact that the culture did not openly advocate for sinful behavior. We now live in a society that is openly seeking to legitimize its sin. Certainly this is not the legacy that you want to leave behind. The *race is not given to the swift or victory to the strong, he that endures to the end shall be saved.* You still have power…you still have influence…you still have a voice. Your family and our nation is not going to get any better unless you use it!

Speak truth freely, while it's still free.

STUDY GUIDE

Chapter 7: GRANDparents

Describe the multigenerational household makeup in many cultures around the world.

What are some of the key pieces of knowledge that grandparents transfer to their grandchildren?

What are some of the factors responsible for the rise in multigenerational households in the United States?

What is the traditional role of grandparents?

What is your nickname for your grandchild; or was your nickname from your grandparents?

Describe a fond memory from your interactions with a grandparent or grandchild.

How has the grandparent role changed in recent years?

How do grandparents provide a menu of the choices of who you might become in life?

Describe the two biblical examples of grandparents in the book.

Are you satisfied with the legacy you are leaving behind? Why or why not?

What does God call grandparents to do if their grandchild refuses to repent and come out of sin? Give scriptural support for your answer.

This book states that "Christian grandparents are the world's last best line of defense against the homosexuality movement." Explain why you agree or disagree with this statement.

Personal take away:

_____

_____

_____

Chapter 8

YOUNG AND RESTLESS

When you were young, and your heart was an open book
You used to say live and let live
But if this ever changing world in which we're living
Makes you give in and cry

Say live and let die
Live and let die
Live and let die
Live and let die

Lyrics from the title song of the 1973 James Bond movie "Live and Let Die"

The song's lyrics provide insight into how our viewpoint changes as we navigate through the stages of life. When teens enter young adulthood, their thinking capacities, relationship skills, and ability to regulate emotions are unlikely to be at a developmental level where they can cope easily with the demands of a diverse, global, technological, rapidly changing world. If all goes well, biology and environment bring a surge of growth paralleling those of childhood and adolescence.

Researchers have begun to define young adulthood as its own developmental period, referring to it as "emerging adulthood," "the frontier of adulthood," or earlier, "the novice phase." Here at the start of the twenty-first century, researchers are creating a new field around young adulthood, just as, at the turn of the twentieth century, researchers defined a new field around adolescence.

Much of the impetus and focus for the research has come from the *lengthening* period in the United States between the onset of puberty and the fulfilling of cultural expectations around adult roles like financial independence and family formation. For the United States, this means that millions of capable late teens and early twenty-something's are *stupidly going where many have gone before* and living to tell about it.

A 1990s survey provided a nationwide sampling of the moral and spiritual perspectives of some five thousand children and adolescents in grades four through twelve. It provides some revealing, and at times disturbing, portraits of how American young people think, act, and view the world. Perhaps the most significant and distinctive feature of the survey is its notion of a "moral compass"—the assumptions that prompt people to choose and behave in certain ways. The survey shows that young people rely on these compasses and make constant use of them. Those who use a "theistic" compass, for instance, base moral decisions and perspectives on the teachings of a religious group or the prevailing norms of a believing community.

Sixteen percent of those surveyed appeared to utilize a theistic compass. African American children and those from lower socioeconomic levels tended more than others to make their decisions from a theistic foundation. According to the survey, 61 percent of children from a theistic orientation claimed they would not cheat on a major test or examination in school, as compared with only 37 percent who used a "utilitarian" compass; 75 percent from a theistic perspective would refuse a drink at a party, as opposed to 50 percent with a "conventionalist" compass (based on accepted social practice) or 33 percent from an "expressivist" ("do what makes me feel good") or utilitarian perspective.

Overall, children who held to a theistic perspective showed greater altruism than those from expressivist or utilitarian orientations. For example, 49 percent of theistic children would set aside their own plans to help a classmate in need, as opposed to 22 percent of utilitarian and 32 percent of expressivist children. Only 6 percent of theistic children would tell a homeless person to get a job, compared to 16 percent of expressivists.

Affluent children showed the greatest uncertainty about what to do and how to act in given circumstances. They were three times more likely not to know how to respond when offered a drink at a party and far less likely to know how or where to begin to advise a friend who became pregnant. Apparently, the greater the wealth, the more extensive the choices, and the more perplexing the world seems to be.

In short, young people's moral perspectives seem to be increasingly diverse and based more on personal experience than on the influence of role models or civic expectations. These figures bear out the premise that, more and more, we are becoming a highly individualistic people, more in tune with our own experiences and ambitions than a common mission or sense of duty.

Over twenty years later, in 2011, the *New York Times* published an article on a major study done at Notre Dame University that sought to determine the values and morals of 230 young adults from across America. The study looked at the young people's moral lives, and the results are depressing. The title of the *Times* article is, "*If it feels right.*"

It's not so much that these young Americans are living lives of sin and debauchery, at least no more than you'd expect from eighteen- to twenty-three-year-olds. What's disheartening is how bad they are at thinking and talking about moral issues. The interviewers asked open-ended questions about right and wrong, moral dilemmas, and the meaning of life. In their rambling answers, the young people were groping to say anything sensible on these matters. They simply did not have the experiences or vocabulary to do so.

They couldn't answer the question or describe problems that are moral at all. They responded with things like, "whether they could afford to rent a certain apartment" or "whether they had enough quarters to feed the meter at a parking spot." Not many of them had previously given much, or any, thought to questions about morality. When asked about wrong or evil, they could generally agree that rape and murder are wrong. But aside from these extreme cases, moral thinking didn't enter the picture, even when considering things like drunken driving, cheating in school, or cheating on a partner.

The default position, which most of them came back to again and again, is that moral choices are just a matter of individual taste. "It's personal," the respondents typically said. "It's up to the individual. Who am I to say?" Rejecting blind deference to authority, many of the young people have gone to the other extreme: "I would do what I thought made me happy or how I felt. I have no other way of knowing what to do but how I internally feel."

Many were quick to talk about their moral feelings but hesitant to link these feelings to any broader thinking about a shared moral framework or obligation. As one put it, "I mean, I guess what makes something right is how I feel about it. But different people feel different ways, so I couldn't speak on behalf of anyone else as to what's right and wrong."

The survey found an atmosphere of extreme moral individualism—of relativism and nonjudgmentalism. Again, **this doesn't mean that America's young people are wholly immoral**. Far from it; they have not been given the resources—by schools, institutions, and families—to cultivate their moral intuitions, to think more broadly about moral obligations, and to check behaviors that may be degrading against an objective moral standard.

*That which has been is what will be, That which is done is what will be done, And there is **nothing new under** the sun* (Eccles. 1:9).

Woe to those who call evil good and good evil, who put darkness for light and light for darkness, who put bitter for sweet and sweet for bitter. ***Woe to those who are wise in their own eyes and clever in their own sight*** (Isa. 5:20–22 [NKJV]).

It is a peculiar circumstance that every generation comes to the conclusion that they have discovered *some new thing* that those before them weren't smart enough or cool enough to figure out. Unfortunately, we live in a world infested with sin, which seems to be more exciting to them. Young people in every age are simply exploring the options, and when they find the boundaries, most of them settle comfortably somewhere inside acceptable social and moral norms.

Human history consistently bears out the fact that societal change often originates with the young generation. In the United States the most recent great change was carried out by young African Americans and young whites. The success of the civil rights movement is due in large part to the collaborative efforts on the part of both groups. Unfortunately, advocates for the homosexual movement have stolen many of the strategies used by the civil rights movement.

The leaders and foot soldiers of the civil rights movement came out of the religious community and saw themselves waging a moral struggle. However, homosexual advocates are advocating for an immoral agenda in an increasingly immoral American climate, especially among the young generation.

In early 2014 the Pew Research Poll conducted a study entitled, "Changing Attitudes on Gay Marriage." The study focused on what is called the millennial generation. Sometimes called Generation Y, and defined by many demographers as ranging from ages eighteen to thirty-seven, they make up the largest population segment the United States has ever seen. Eighty-six-million strong, it is 7 percent larger than the baby-boom generation, which came of age in the 1970s and '80s. And the millennial population could keep growing to 88.5 million people by 2020, owing to immigration.

The study showed that 64 percent of millennials and 55 percent of generation X (born 1965–1980) favor or do not oppose homosexual marriage. The majority of Republicans ages eighteen to twenty-nine think gays and lesbians should be allowed to marry, according to a Pew Research poll, while a majority of Democrats regardless of age supports gay marriage.

Republican views divide strikingly along generational lines, with support dropping precipitously among older members of the party. The youngest segment is nearly three times more likely to support gay marriage than those sixty-five and over. Just 18 percent of Republicans under thirty said that more gay and lesbian couples raising children is a bad thing, compared to about half of those ages thirty to sixty-four and 66 percent of those sixty-five and older.

Overall backing for gay marriage continues to grow, with some pollsters finding support now nearing 60 percent. Although gay-rights issues have been prominent in the news lately, they went virtually unmentioned at the last (2014) Conservative Political Action Conference, where a majority of attendees were under twenty-five. One twenty-two-year-old student stated, "Most of my friends just think it's not an issue."

The focus of this writing has been to bring clarity to the issue of the expanding homosexual movement. But, the greater intent is to serve as a clarion call to the eroding moral fiber of our nation. The founding fathers agreed that our freedom documents were *meant for a moral people,* that they were totally inadequate for an immoral electorate because such a society is in more need of masters and is not able to rule themselves. That is the reason the Frenchman Alex de Tocqueville in 1850 said that he found the secret to America's success in her schools and churches, where God's Word and laws, morality, freedom, and personal responsibility were taught.

The twentieth century brought many significant changes for American society. One such change was the idea that as time passes, the United States is being molded and shaped by generational groups. The first such definable group was the "baby boomers." Baby boomers are people born between the years 1946 and 1964.

Baby boomers are associated with a rejection or redefinition of traditional values; on the other hand, many history commentators have disputed the extent of that rejection, noting the widespread continuity of values between older and younger generations. As a group, boomers were the wealthiest, most active, and most physically fit generation up to that time, and among the first to grow up genuinely expecting the world to improve with time.

Generally, boomers expected to work, marry, and raise a family. Obviously not everyone shared the same religious beliefs; yet they did share a common position on the sanctity of the home. In the eyes of most people, the home was to be undisturbed;

free from violation, injury or desecration. Societal laws, customs, and traditions were designed to protect, defend, and further the traditional family unit. Boomers envisioned communities where husbands (men) and wives (women) would rear their children in a morally, wholesome climate. Moreover, they envisioned the time when they would pass this hope and vision on to their children's children.

Baby boomers are entering their twilight years and handing the reigns of authority and influence over to generation X and millennials. The United States that they are handing over is very different from the one they grew up in and raised their children in. Boomers had the luxury of being *young and restless* in a time when youthful indiscretions were overlooked. They were overlooked primarily for three reasons:

1. The effects of their actions were usually insignificant and short-lived
2. There was an expectation that the young person would shortly mature beyond this stage
3. Society as a whole functioned to maintain and reinforce the agreed upon moral codes

For millennials and generation Z (those born after millennials), ignorance is no longer bliss (if it ever was). The United States that you are inheriting is not as kind and gentle as it once was. The United States of your grandparents youth was built around TV shows such as *Father Knows Best, Leave It To Beaver,* and *The Waltons.* That TV generation has given way to primetime lineups built around themes of inept husbands, promiscuous housewives, and homosexual family units, all delivered under the label of a *Modern Family* and a *New Normal.* The United States of today is bearing the fruits of past generations that sought to loosen the restraints on the pursuit of their passions.

Your America is wrestling with issues that regularly happen at a frequency your parents and grandparents never dreamed of: rape, murder, sexual assault, child predators, registered sex offenders, and the free and open expression of homosexuality as just another lifestyle choice. Add to this the brokenness resulting from fragmented families, and culturally you have a society where millions of millennials and generation Z simply don't have the proper framework for a healthy biblical marriage. In far too many of their lives, pornography has desensitized their desire for a real woman or man, creating the danger that sex will become a single-person, private act.

Coupled with this phenomenon, divorce has shattered their view of traditional marriage, and many have replaced it with a notion of romantic love that's loosely solidified in cohabitation. For far too many, marriage has lost its sacredness, and social scientists are writing that we must prepare for a postmarriage culture. Unmarried Millennials and generation Z, as you look five, seven, or ten years down the road to the time when you will be looking to settle down and start a family, this is the America that awaits you and your first born.

Where will you find the wholesome communities like those in which your parents raised you and your grandparents raised your parents? Will your children be able to go over to the next street and play with their friends? Or will you only allow them to play in the cul de sac, and then only as long as you can keep a watchful eye on them? Or will you make them wear electronic monitors with GPS tracking that will allow you to know where they are, and in the worst case scenario will allow the authorities to locate them?

If you are indeed *young and restless,* there is a ball game or party to go to, and you are probably not at all trying to have these kinds of thoughts at this point in your life. You know what, neither your parents nor grandparents were having these thoughts at your age, either. But they had a different America than the one that you will bring your children into.

Baby boomers and their big-band sound gave way to rock and roll, which gave way to disco that has given way to hip hop; can you imagine what's next? To Millennials and generation Z: ***I am truly sorry, America can't afford for you to finish sowing your wild oats.*** The moral degradation that has occurred over the past thirty to forty years is far too great for the country to wait until you finish *your turn.*

In five or ten years, our nation will not magically become morally pure just because you decide to grow up, settle down, and act like a responsible adult. *Here's the deal:* If you want a more moral nation when you are ready to raise a family, you must start building it today. That third leg of support that your grandfather had during his roaring twenties has suffered severe erosion: "3. society as a whole functioned to maintain and reinforce the mutually agreed upon moral codes." In fact, we no longer have a mutual moral agreement.

The politically correct standard of today is *if it feels good to you, just do it!* Today there are many immoral voices speaking up for their positions, but legalized immorality will never be right in the sight of God and will never improve the moral condition of mankind.

For if you remain completely silent at this time, relief and deliverance will arise for the Jews from another place, but you and your father's house will perish. ***Yet who knows whether you have come to the kingdom for such a time as this*** (Esther 4:14 [NKJV])?

During the time of Esther, the nation of Israel was in a great crisis. As the result of a wicked scheme by Haman, all Jews were going to be annihilated. In the verse above, her cousin Mordecai is trying to convince Esther to risk her life by going in, without a request, and appeal to the king to save the Jews. Mordecai reassures her that God's people will be delivered; however, she and her father's house may very well perish if she refuses to speak to the king. Esther finds the courage to go in and her people are saved.

Although the current threat isn't as imminent as that facing the Jews in the book of Esther, the United States is definitely under a growing crisis. The level of immorality openly displayed in society today likely would have been unfathomable to most Americans living just fifty years ago. And if all of us don't start to address it now, only God knows what our nation will look like fifty years from now.

Millennials and generarion Z, maybe, just maybe, *you were born for such a time as this.*

Speak truth freely, while it's still free.

STUDY GUIDE

Chapter 8: Young and Restless

Describe some of the environmental factors impacting young people as they enter and travel through the developmental period known as 'young adulthood.'

What are some of the potential impacts on society related to the lengthening period in the United States between the onset of puberty and the fulfilling of cultural expectations around adult roles?

What were some of the outcomes of the survey on teenagers' moral compasses?

The survey concluded that young people's moral perspectives are based primarily on _____ and _____ rather than on role models or civic expectations. Fill in the blanks and discuss the implications.

What are some of the findings of the 2011 Notre Dame young-adult survey?

Why did the 2011 survey conclude that there exists among young people an atmosphere of extreme moral individualism—of relativism and nonjudgmentalism? Discuss your agreement or disagreement.

Describe how Isaiah 5:20–22 relates to both surveys' findings about young people.

Discuss some of the historical societal changes that have originated with the younger generation.

Describe how millennials and generation Xers view homosexual marriage.

Discuss the recent opinion shifts on homosexual marriage by Republicans.

What were Alex de Tocqueville's concluding thoughts about America?

Describe the typical life and expectations of a baby boomer.

Describe the United States that millennials and generation Xers are inheriting from baby boomers.

Discuss why the United States can't afford for millennials and generation Z to finish their turn at sowing their wild oats.

Generation X, millennials and generation Z, were you born for such a time as this? Why or why not?

Personal take away:

_____

_____

_____

Chapter 9

IN CONCLUSION: WHO WILL GO?

I said to myself, "Come now, be merry; enjoy yourself to the full." But I found that this, too, was futile. For it is silly to be laughing all the time; what good does it do? So after a lot of thinking, I decided to try the road of drink, while still holding steadily to my course of seeking wisdom. Next I changed my course again and followed the path of folly, so that I could experience the only happiness most men have throughout their lives (Eccles. 2:1–3 [TLB]).

The book of Ecclesiastes was written by Solomon, who was a king of Israel and the son of David. The conventional dates of Solomon's reign are around 970 to 931 BC. He was the third king of the United Monarchy and the final king before the northern Kingdom of Israel and the southern Kingdom of Judah split. Following the split, his patrilineal (line of David) descendants ruled over Judah alone.

The Bible credits Solomon as the builder of the First Temple in Jerusalem and portrays him as great in wisdom, wealth, and power, but ultimately as a king whose sin, including idolatry and turning away from God, leads to the kingdom being torn in two during the reign of his son Rehoboam. In his quest to find true happiness Solomon did not deny himself any pleasure this world had to offer. Throughout his lifetime he partook of much *wine, women, and song,* and topped it off with wisdom, knowledge, and power. He was the wisest and richest man of his time, but he engaged in fleshly lusts that led to his heart being turned from God.

Like Solomon, the United States is engaging in sins of the flesh that are turning millions of hearts from God. Chief among these sins, homosexuality is causing tremendous harm to God's design for the home. Homosexual activists have coopted politicians and judges to make laws and render judicial decisions that grant two men the same rights and privileges as God's holy institution of marriage, which is designed for a man and a woman.

But, my son be warned: there is no end of opinions ready to be expressed. Studying them can go on forever and become very exhausting (Eccles. 12:12 [TLB])!

Today millions of Americans have been swayed by the *opinions* expressed by some academics, lay persons, and religious scholars. These thought leaders have written, spoken, and preached the lie that a loving God would never deny anyone the right to be in a marital relationship with whoever is the object of his or her sincere affections. They have perverted and corrupted God's principles in their efforts to find legitimacy and open expression of a debase lifestyle. But, the fact remains that what God has forbidden is not a matter that's up for debate. Our safety and salvation lie in complete submission to the will of God without question.

The material in this book is designed to inform and inspire people of faith. You have read many scriptures explaining God's design, along with many accounts of humans' actions throughout the history of the world. Now, *in conclusion*, how should God's true followers respond to this present wave of evil? Are they resigned to helplessly be swept along by the currents of public opinion and political correctness?

Humanity, especially young people, has always tested the limits of God's authority. Solomon's life story stands for all time as an example of the fact that as long as you are alive, it is never too late to change course. Everyone who practices sin and lawlessness is capable of repentance and restoration. As it was with Adam and Eve, humans have always been intrigued by the things that God has forbidden. At the same time, God has always allowed mankind free will to choose to disobey him and then given man time to repent and change his life course.

The Lord is not slack concerning his promise, as some count slackness, but is longsuffering toward us, not willing that any should perish but that all should come to repentance (2 Pet. 3:9 [NKJV]).

*Here is **my final conclusion:** fear God and obey his commandments, for this is the entire duty of man. For God will judge us for everything we do, including every hidden thing, good or bad* (Eccles. 12:13–14 [TLB]).

If homosexuals are to repent and turn from their sin, someone has to stand up and *speak the truth in love* to them. Christians do not have the luxury of going along to get along on this or any other issue where God has said people must not engage. This does not mean that you have to set out at once in search of personal confrontations; however, it is well past time for the Christian community to speak in a unified voice.

If you have read this book in its entirety, you are to be commended. Thank you. Your interest in spiritual matters and your diligence to seek information is commendable. Now, this is the point where the rubber meets the road. You are nearing the end, and the question that we all must answer is almost upon you. This book stands as my personal answer to this question. In all of human history, whenever evil is to be put down, God has asked, **"Who will go?"**

In Conclusion: Who Will Go?

*And he touched my mouth with it (a burning coal), and said, "Behold, this has touched your lips; Your iniquity is taken away, And your sin purged." Also I heard the voice of the Lord, saying: "Whom shall I send, And who will go for Us?" Then I said, "**Here am I! Send me.**" And he said, "Go, and tell this people:…"* (Isa. 6:7–9a [NKJV]).

Although we are not called to be prophets, we are called to speak out against evil. *How we speak, when we speak, where we speak, and who we speak to is left up to us.* However, the decision to speak is not optional. You must say something, to somebody, at some point.

In the first century AD, the Jews were in an uproar because Christians sought to bring about change by preaching the gospel of Christ and demanding that people turn away from every false way and submit to the Son of God by rendering obedience to His gospel. Christians were accused of turning the world upside down. Sharing the gospel brought about controversy and resulted in public confrontation.

These early disciples were not afraid nor did they shun controversy. They knew that being a Christian obligated them to take up their cross and follow after Christ. Being a Christian also required that they preached the gospel to every person that they came across and defended that gospel against attacks made on it. In the first century, the options were very clear; you were either with Jesus or against him.

Then Jesus said to His disciples, "If anyone desires to come after me, let him deny himself, and take up his cross, and follow me. For whoever desires to save his life will lose it, but whoever loses his life for my sake will find it" (Matt. 16:24–25 [NKJV]).

Those who argue or imply that the scriptures must be "adapted," "modified," or "changed" in any way to embrace our postmodern culture are guilty of casting reflection upon the wisdom and power of almighty God. It was God who made humans. Does he not know humans better than humans know themselves? Could he not give people a gospel that is relevant to all people's needs in all ages of time?

To deny that he could is to expose one's lack of understanding of the gospel and one's lack of faith in God's all-powerful, all-knowing, and benevolent nature. There is but one gospel, one moral and spiritual standard for all humankind. The moral standards of Christianity are for all people for all time. Any human behavior that is not in harmony with that standard must be reproved, rejected, and condemned.

God has so ordered our world that humankind is free to live as they wish, in complete and total disobedience to God's moral standards. And without a doubt, if people refuse to repent and exit this life with their sins unforgiven, they cannot and will not escape God's final judgment:

*For we must all appear before the **judgment** seat of Christ; that every one may receive the things done in his body, according to that he hath done, whether it be good or bad* (2 Cor. 5:10).

In the book of Jonah, God calls him to go and prophesy to the city of Nineveh so that its inhabitants might turn from their sin and be saved. Jonah did not want to go to Nineveh; he did not want them to be spared. He tried to escape from God; but, in the end he went, and Nineveh was saved from destruction. Can you think of anything more unloving than to see lost souls and not give them an opportunity to repent and receive God's salvation? Out of love, Christians are exhorted to ...*contend earnestly for the faith*... (Jude 3) that the world might turn from their sin and live.

Genuine Christian love for truth leads a person into being in opposition to anything that would rival the truth. The motive of Christians in engaging the world and speaking against sin is not

In Conclusion: Who Will Go?

to condemn the world. When Christians insist that the scriptures must be obeyed, it is out of love for God and people. *Thou shalt love the Lord thy God with all thy heart and with all thy soul and with thy entire mind…and…thou shalt love thy neighbor as thyself* (Matt. 22:37–39 [NKJV]). God's love inspires believers to give their all to win obedience for the Master, whereby God offers a pardon to those who will repent and obey.

Then Jesus said to His disciples (followers), "If anyone desires to come after me, let him deny himself, and take up his cross, and follow me. For whoever desires to save his life will lose it, but whoever loses his life for my sake will find it. For what profit is it to a man if he gains the whole world, and loses his own soul? Or what will a man give in exchange for his soul?" (Matt. 16:24–26 [(NKJV]).

Go therefore and make disciples of all the nations, baptizing them in the name of the Father and of the Son and of the Holy Spirit, teaching them to observe all things that I have commanded you; and lo, I am with you always, even to the end of the age. Amen (Matt. 28:19–20 [NKJV]).

We must go and tell them that the God of heaven does indeed love them and wants them to be happy. Yet, more than that, he wants them to live in obedience to His Word. Tell them the most fulfilling and rewarding life that humankind can live is one lived in accordance with the will of God found in the holy scriptures.

The goal of this book is to honestly, lovingly, and most important, correctly present the Bible's position on homosexuality. It was written for the purpose of being a conversation starter to get Christians talking outside of the safe confines of the church building. If the United States is to turn from its current path of immorality and become a nation that's seeking to live righteously, it is Christians who must lead the way by shining as marvelous lights in this present age of darkness.

Homosexual advocates have been advocating for the past thirty to forty years, seeking a change in societal norms and enacting laws to bring legitimacy to their deviant lifestyle. Thus far they have operated largely unopposed or at least without a unified opposition from the Christian community. It is well past time for a countermovement. God is calling Christians to let their lights shine in the presence of this current darkness *(Mat 5:15)*.

The challenge for Christians today is to rediscover a sense of disgust and outrage:

[Jesus Cleanses the Temple] Then Jesus went into the temple of God and drove out all those who bought and sold in the temple, and overturned the tables of the money changers and the seats of those who sold doves (Matt. 21:12 [NKJV]).

Can you picture this scene? Jesus is acting like a wild man, turning over tables and driving people out of the room. Is this the same Jesus who wept with compassion at the death of his friend Lazarus (John 11:28–36)? Is this the same Jesus who wept over Jerusalem (Luke 19:41–42)? Yes, it is! He is demonstrating that we ought not to allow anything to rule over our *righteous indignation* at the actions of those who willfully disobey and disrespect God.

Have we allowed this world to redefine outrageous behavior? In the world's view lust of the *flesh, lust of the eyes and the pride of life* are normal pursuits (1 John 2:16). This world has redefined homosexuality as a normal lifestyle in which two men or women are free to fall in love, marry, and raise a family. We must see the world through God's eyes, which will enable us to rediscover our own personal sense of disgust and outrage. When we see the world through God's eyes, we will possess the righteous indignation whereby we will find the courage to speak and to act.

In Conclusion: Who Will Go?

Christians are called to live in the world and not to be of the world (John 17:14). We are called to be *wise as serpents, yet gentle as doves* (Matt. 10:16). Therefore, Christians must understand how power and influence works in the world and utilize this process to further the cause of righteousness. During the last generation, homosexual advocates learned this and used it to fuel a movement away from the godly foundation of marriage upon which our nation was established.

Throughout the Old Testament, Israel demonstrated that a nation is always one generation away from change. As it was with Israel, so it can be with the United States. But, movements don't just happen. They are orchestrated and carried out by *advocates* who are seeking a change in the status quo. What are you advocating for by the way you are living your life?

Every day you go out into the world and advocate for something simply by the way you live. The way you dress, what you eat, and definitely your speech tell others what you are advocating for. **Christians are called to be God's advocates in the world**, and the United States is in desperate need of a back-to-morality movement. There is no better time than now for you to become an advocate for the change you are seeking.

In conclusion, will you go?

Speak truth freely, while it's still free.

STUDY GUIDE

Chapter 9: In Conclusion: Who Will Go?

Describe King Solomon's journey to find happiness.

Is it possible for men/women to pursue their fleshly passions and maintain a heart for God? Why or why not?

Discuss how Ecclesiastes 12:12 relates to the things written/spoken today in support of the homosexual movement.

How would you describe the condition of men's heart in Genesis 6:5 and Proverbs 6:14 with today? What are the implications for our current society?

How would you explain why God has allowed humankind to test the limits of his authority?

What must happen if homosexuals are to repent and turn from their sin?

Sharing the gospel in the world will inevitably produce _____ and _____.

Are the moral standards of Christianity for all people for all time? Why or why not?

What is the proper motive for Christians to engage the world and speak the truth against sin?

Has God given Christians the authority to speak against sin in the world? Give scriptural support for your answer.

Regarding those living in sin, has God mandated **when** we speak, where we speak, and who we speak to?

Describe what righteous indignation looks like. Have you ever expressed it or personally seen it expressed?

How do "movements" start and who is responsible for their success?

If someone examined your life, what would he or she conclude you are an advocate for? (Rhetorical question intended for personal contemplation only)

Personal take away:

_____

_____

_____

Chapter 10

GREATER WORKS THAN THESE

Moral conditions in our nation are declining. The goal of this writing has been to present the circumstances of the day fairly and truthfully. And the truth is God's people took a nap for the past thirty years, and homosexual advocates devised a plan and went to work. They have gone largely unchallenged, and it's little wonder people of faith find themselves on the verge of being silenced. They have all but silenced the politicians from both major parties, and they've coopted judges who are over turning state constitutional amendments established by the will of the people to outlaw same-sex marriage.

In our wildest dreams, who would have ever thought that in the United States of America we would need to establish a constitutional amendment to outlaw marriage between two men or two women, and after doing so, a judge entrusted to uphold the will of the people would overturn the amendment and grant legal sanction to this ungodly union? Yet in 2014, this is indeed the predicament in which our nation finds itself.

Nothing can resist the human will that will stake even its existence on its stated purpose.

Benjamin Disraeli

Most assuredly, I say to you, he who believes in me, the works that I do he will do also; and **greater works than these he will do***, because I go to my Father. And whatever you ask in my name, that I will do, that the Father may be glorified in the Son. If you ask anything in my name, I will do it* (John 14:12–14 [NKJV]).

Again I say to you that if two of you agree on earth concerning anything that they ask, it will be done for them by my Father in heaven. For where two or three are gathered together in my name, I am there in the midst of them (Matt. 18:19–20 ([NKJV]).

It is certainly undeniable that we have some grave challenges before us. Are they insurmountable? Far from it! The key element in the quote by Benjamin Disraeli is "the will of the people." Thus far the will of God's people hasn't been mobilized against the immoral revolution engulfing our nation. And when the will of the people is united in God's will nothing can stand against them. Throughout the Bible, and human history, all successful campaigns for righteousness needed only two things:

1. A God-approved plan of action and,
2. The will of the people to act

Later in this chapter you will read a proposed plan of action to speak against the current immoral revolution. Some people will disagree because they don't think it's a good plan and don't believe it will ever work. To them I say; ask yourself if it is a better plan than the one Joshua had at Jericho (Josh. Chapter 6). Their plan was to have the priests and men of war march around the wall and on the seventh day blow a horn. Can't you hear some of the people asking: "Are you absolutely sure you heard God correctly?"

Lao Tzu wrote, *a journey of a thousand miles begins with the first step.* You have taken the first step by reading this book. If you've read the entirety to this point, you have encountered enough information to successfully refute anyone who'd dare try to defend homosexuality on any level. If you weren't familiar with some of the scriptural content, take some time to go back and study and meditate on them.

As your study group assembled weekly to discuss each chapter, hopefully everyone grew in knowledge and confidence, and you all have formed a bond of unity to stand and speak truth freely in support of God's holy institution of marriage. Fair warning: when you do speak, be prepared for a swift rebuttal. A short while ago, one member of the family behind the TV show *Duck Dynasty* spoke up. Although he may not have spoken eloquently, he did speak truthfully in regards to homosexuality being a sin:

Duck Dynasty star suspended for antigay remarks (excerpts from news reports)

Phil Robertson, a star of A&E's *Duck Dynasty*, has been suspended indefinitely after slamming gays in a magazine interview. In an interview in the January 2014 issue of GQ, Robertson says homosexuality is a sin and puts it in the same category as bestiality and promiscuity. "We are extremely disappointed to have read Phil Robertson's comments in GQ, which are based on his own personal beliefs and are not reflected in the series *Duck Dynasty*," the network said in a statement. "His personal views in no way reflect those of A&E Networks, who have always been strong supporters and champions of the LGBT community. The network has placed Phil under hiatus from filming indefinitely."

Fans, Foes React to *Duck Dynasty* Star Phil Robertson's Reinstatement

Reactions are pouring in to the A&E Network's reversal of *Duck Dynasty* hero Phil Robertson's "indefinite" suspension for his comments against homosexuality. While fans remain uncertain of A&E's "true intent," opponents say they'll be watching carefully the show's next steps. The decision by A&E to reinstate Robertson "is in direct response to the powerful and engaged voices of millions of Faith Driven Consumers, as highlighted by more than 260,000 signers of the IStandWithPhil.com petition," the advocacy group noted in a statement. But Faith Driven Consumers added that the question whether their community has truly been heard still remains unanswered.

Family Research Council (FRC) President Tony Perkins said the return of Robertson in the face of backlash "is quite telling to the American people who are growing tired of GLAAD and cultural elites who want to silence people and remove God and His Word from every aspect of public life." GLAAD, formerly the Gay & Lesbian Alliance Against Defamation, campaigned against Robertson's comments, which contributed to A&E's decision to suspend the conservative Christian.

"The attacks on Phil Robertson revealed to the American people that the push to redefine marriage is less about the marriage altar than it is fundamentally altering America's moral, political and cultural landscape," Perkins said in a statement.

GLAAD seeks to silence "anyone who dare challenge the idea that homosexuality is normal," Perkins added. "However, the Robertson family's refusal to cower to GLAAD's bullying and the ensuing backlash to the suspension, unlike anything since Chick-fil-A Appreciation Day, finally forced A&E Network to withdraw the suspension."

Why did A&E reverse its course? Did they suddenly *get religion*? Of course not, they reinstated Phil Robertson because "we the people" stood up and spoke in one united voice. If we learned nothing else, we learned that when the people speak in unison, television executives listen. What do you think would have happened if the people had not spoken? No need to answer that.

To be sure, there are executives at A&E who agree with the Bible and Phil Robertson. In addition, many would agree that Christians have the same free speech rights as those advocating for the homosexual agenda. But what other position could they have taken before "we the people" spoke up? We have to understand that no one in a position of authority will move against this present force of political correctness unless we the people demonstrate that we will support them when the protesters and news media show up. They need to know that we will be there to help them fight to keep their job.

Consider this recent example that occurred in Arizona:

Arizona governor Jan Brewer vetoed a bill that would have allowed businesses that asserted their religious beliefs the right to deny service to gay and lesbian customers. The controversial measure faced a surge of opposition in recent days from large corporations and athletic organizations, including Delta Air Lines, the Super Bowl host committee, and Major League Baseball.

Fiercely divided supporters and opponents of the bill ramped up pressure on Brewer after the state's Republican-led legislature approved it last week. The governor said she made the decision she knew was right for Arizona. "I call them as I see them, despite the cheers or the boos from the crowd," Brewer said, criticizing what she described as a "broadly worded" bill that "could result in unintended and negative consequences."

Brewer said she'd weighed the arguments on both sides before vetoing the measure: "To the supporters of the legislation, I want you to know that I understand that long-held norms about marriage and family are being challenged as never before. Our society is undergoing many dramatic changes. However, I sincerely believe that Senate Bill 1062 has the potential to create more problems than it purports to solve. It could divide Arizona in ways we cannot even imagine and no one would ever want. Religious liberty is a core American and Arizona value. So is nondiscrimination."

We the people must understand that this isn't a fad. Homosexual advocates aren't going to go away just because we find them unpleasant. The Arizona effort showed us that there are politicians who are willing to take the lead and seek to recover some of the ground we have lost; but we must take the first step. *Duck Dynasty* showed us that we will speak when they get our full attention. Fortunately or unfortunately, it took *messing* with one of our favorite TV shows to engage us after a thirty-year period of severe attention deficit.

For everyone who desires to restore America to a moral high ground, the next step is for all of us to walk the talk. In the comfort of our private enclaves, we all bravely decry the growing immorality in our nation. But who is willing to go public? Who's willing to take a stand and be outed as a Christian? The intent here is not to brow beat anyone; taking a public stance against any immoral behavior in this climate of tolerance for everything isn't easy. So what's the answer?

Is the answer intolerance? Before you answer let's define tolerance: *having a permissive attitude toward opinions and practices that differ from one's own (Random House).* We are currently living with the results of far too many Americans having a permissive attitude toward those who want to live a public life of homosexuality and enjoy all the rights and privileges of holy matrimony.

Let's consider intolerance: *lack of toleration; unwillingness or refusal to tolerate or respect contrary opinions or beliefs (Random House).*

The problem with this word is that people of faith have allowed the world to define how we should apply the meaning to our life. They say the word applies to us universally, meaning that we are holistically either tolerant of everything or intolerant of everything.

What an absurd conclusion. Good people, we have been *bamboozled*. Everyone is tolerant of some things and intolerant of others. Some people are tolerant of X, while others won't tolerate it at all. Some people are tolerant of Y, while others won't tolerate it in the least. Christians should have about as much tolerance for homosexuality as God does: *You shall not lie with a male as with a woman. It is an abomination* (Lev. 18:22 [NKJV]). At all times Christians must speak the truth in love (Eph. 4:15), and after doing so, if someone concludes that you are an intolerant bigot, be at ease because you are in good company.

Back to the question at hand, are **you** willing to walk the talk? It is said that there is security in numbers; if so would you feel secure if your voice was one of one million people who are taking a stand against the growing immorality invading our nation? How secure would you feel if you showed up for a public event in support of God's view of marriage, and there were 999,999 other people there? Would this be enough security to get you to show up?

This book is part of a broader effort to launch a grassroots campaign to improve our nation's moral climate. Please go to *www.SpeakTruthFreely.com* and add your voice to others who have decided to stand up and speak truth freely. Think about it: 260,000 people signed an online petition and caused a national television network to reverse its decision and rule against the desires of homosexual advocates.

What could one million motivated God-fearing Americans accomplish? Could they convince the FCC to reduce the amount of sexuality, profanity, and violence allowed in prime time network and cable TV shows? Could they put enough public pressure on federal judges to convince them to stop overturning state constitutional amendments where the people have voted against same-sex marriage? Maybe they could persuade corporate CEOs to allow work environments to be places where Christian viewpoints are *tolerated* and allowed free and open expression? Maybe they could establish a national Christian counseling hotline for teens who are confused and struggling with their sexuality (staffed by professional Christian counselors)?

How do we get from today's reality to this very realistic future? One person, one household at a time! As it was with Joshua, so it must be with every one of us: *And if it seems evil to you to serve the Lord, choose for yourselves this day whom you will serve, whether the gods which your fathers served that were on the other side of the river, or the gods of the Amorites, in whose land you dwell.* **But as for me and my house, we will serve the Lord** (Josh. 24:15 [NKJV]).

The hope for this book is that it has increased your knowledge of the Bible, equipped you to defend what you believe, and given you the faith and the courage to act. As Christians, our charge is to first get right ourselves, and then be a light for others to find their way out of the darkness: *Let your light so shine before men, that they may see your good works and glorify your Father in heaven* (Matt. 5:16 [NKJV]). This is a pretty simple mission. Unfortunately, people have artificially complicated many of God's truths.

Humankind represents the crowning achievement of God's creation; in fact, he made man a little lower than the angels and given him free will. Almost from creation humans have taken this freedom to question God and sometimes elevate themselves above him. However, when we read Genesis, chapter one, we find that there are thirty-one verses, and God is mentioned thirty-two times. It doesn't take a genius to correctly conclude that it's not about us.

God has given humans free will, which they may use to follow the desires of their hearts and live any way they want. God will one day welcome into his eternal rest those who have steadfastly lived a life of faithful obedience to his truth. For those who have taken this freedom to live a crooked and perverse life, God has promised to one day exact judgment upon them. Although his love and mercy will take no pleasure in it, his justice will demand that they spend eternity *weeping and gnashing their teeth* (Matt. 13:42).

But there is hope. Christians are the ones charged with delivering this hope to a lost and dying world: *Go therefore and make disciples of all the nations, baptizing them in the name of the Father and of the Son and of the Holy Spirit,* **teaching them to observe all things that I have commanded you;**... (Matt. 28:19–20a [NKJV]). As Christians, we must *observe all things that have been commanded* by God and seek to influence those living outside the commands to render obedience before it is too late. May it never be said that a child of God chose **silence** over the risk of offending someone who might have been ready to lay down the yoke of sin and obey the truth.

Please, speak truth freely, WHETHER IT'S FREE OR NOT!

STUDY GUIDE

Chapter 10: Greater Works than These

Among the many gains by homosexual advocates, what are you most troubled by?

What is the quote by Benjamin Disraeli? Do you think this is true or just a nice quote?

If a homosexual advocate was motivated by this quote, how might he/she be feeling today?

No offense to Benjamin Disraeli, but what is possible for God's people who truly believe and are motivated by John 14:12–14 and Matthew 18:19–20?

What are the two things this book gives that are necessary for a successful campaign for righteousness? Explain why you agree or disagree.

Describe the key action that caused A&E to change their position on Phil Robertson.

Describe the plan of action that led to the defeat of Arizona State Senate Bill 1062.

What does the world mean when it binds "tolerance" upon all citizens?

Is God intolerant of homosexuality? Scripturally support your answer.

What could one million motivated God-fearing Americans accomplish in stemming the tide of immorality and restore the lost respect for God and his word?

Last question:

Are you willing to be outed as a Christian for speaking God's truth freely? If your answer is yes, sign up at *www.speaktruthfreely.com*. If your answer is no, keep studying God's Word and pray for those who answered yes.

Personal take away:

_____

_____

_____